China – Politics and Economics

edited by

Prof. Dr. Doris Fischer
Prof. Dr. Jörn-Carsten Gottwald
Dr. Katja Levy

Volume 4

Katja Levy | Annette Zimmer | Qingyu Ma (eds.)

Still a Century of Corporatism?

Models of State-Society Cooperation
in China and Germany

 Nomos

This research project was generously funded by the Stiftung Mercator (Project No. 155300).

STIFTUNG
MERCATOR

The Deutsche Nationalbibliothek lists this publication in the Deutsche Nationalbibliografie; detailed bibliographic data are available on the Internet at http://dnb.d-nb.de

ISBN   978-3-8487-6602-4 (Print)
            978-3-7489-0740-4 (ePDF)

British Library Cataloguing-in-Publication Data
A catalogue record for this book is available from the British Library.

ISBN   978-3-8487-6602-4 (Print)
            978-3-7489-0740-4 (ePDF)

Library of Congress Cataloging-in-Publication Data
Levy, Katja / Zimmer, Annette / Ma, Qingyu
Still a Century of Corporatism?
Models of State-Society Cooperation in China and Germany
Katja Levy / Annette Zimmer / Qingyu Ma (eds.)
185 pp.
Includes bibliographic references.

ISBN   978-3-8487-6602-4 (Print)
            978-3-7489-0740-4 (ePDF)

Onlineversion
Nomos eLibrary

1st Edition 2021
© Nomos Verlagsgesellschaft, Baden-Baden, Germany 2021. Overall responsibility for manufacturing (printing and production) lies with Nomos Verlagsgesellschaft mbH & Co. KG.

Table of Contents

Introduction

Katja Levy, Annette Zimmer, Qingyu Ma

This volume assembles scholarly papers[1] that represent part of the results of a three-year research project ("LoGoSO Project"[2]) in Germany and China. Earlier versions of these articles were presented at the annual conference of ARNOVA[3] in San Diego in November 2019. This introduction aims to unfurl the background to this comparative project, including the larger discussion on corporatism, and explicate the methodology which we applied in this project. In the final section of this chapter, we will give a short overview of the six contributions to the book.

Background to the Project—Migration, a Challenge for Local Governments

When we started the LoGoSO project in 2016, we were puzzled by two things. First, we wanted to know more about the challenges posed by migration to local governments in China and Germany. In the previous year, Germany had experienced an influx of migrants from war-ridden countries of historical dimensions. These people had been turned down by other European states and were now looking for shelter in the country that had kept its door open. China was not much affected by these events but had experienced several migration generations of even larger dimensions since the 1980s. At that time, the Chinese government had introduced *Reform*

---

1 The authors would like to thank Mark Sidel, Hu Yinglian, Christina Maags and other participants in the ARNOVA annual conference and the Annual Meeting of the Working Group of Social Science Researchers on China (ASC) of the German Association for Asian Studies in 2019 for their very helpful comments on the contributions.

2 LoGoSO stands for *local government-social organisation*; the full name of the project is: Models of cooperation between Local Governments and Social Organizations—Migration: Challenges and Opportunities. The project received funding from the Stiftung Mercator. The word social organisation is used interchangeably with non-profit organisation in this volume. The word social organisation is mostly used in research literature on the Chinese third sector.

3 Association for Research on Nonprofit Organizations and Voluntary Action.

and Opening policies and (informally) relaxed the household registration system.[4] It had thus enabled rural inhabitants to move to the cities to find work in the fast-growing manufacturing and assembling factories in the country's eastern coastal areas. We were eager to understand better the challenges that migration entails for local governments and their response to them. Secondly, we wanted to map and explain recent transformations in state–society relations. As we will discuss below, Germany is just growing out of its corporatist traditions. And we found that in China corporatism is being similarly replaced with neoliberal concepts of efficient service provision.

Thus, the research project wishes to compare Germany and China in three main respects: How are the local governments in both countries affected by the influx of large numbers of migrants? How do the local governments respond to these extraordinary challenges? And, what role do non-profit organisations, as providers of public services[5], play in this historically unique situation?

The Challenges of Migration

The LoGoSO project juxtaposes two countries faced with challenging migration movements, albeit very different ones. Germany received migrants from different countries and cultural backgrounds; China experienced do-

---

4 The PRC government introduced the household registration (户口 *hukou*) system in the 1950s. In the early years of the People's Republic, it had the purpose of controlling rural migration to the cities and was strictly implemented. It meant that citizens with rural *hukou* who nevertheless came to the cities had an illegal status and were not eligible for any public services. Health insurance for themselves and their families or schooling for the children at a place different to their registered home were out of reach. When economic development took off in the 1980s and workers were needed in the industrial areas along the east coast of China, the implementation of the *hukou* regulations was relaxed, but only to a certain degree. Workers were able to move to the cities with less risk of being sent back home but still without access to social services for themselves and their families. More recently, migrant workers in the cities have had limited access to social services at their place of work. Since the social security systems of China's rural and urban areas were strictly separated, the reform of these systems and the ensuing reform of the *hukou* system are complex processes that are still going on.

5 Public services refer to services provided to needy members of society. These services can be considered part of the responsibility of the state but are outsourced to other organisations, non-profit organisations (or social organisations) or for-profit organisations.

mestic migration from one locality within the country to another. However, from a more abstract point of view, the two countries faced similar challenges, particularly at the local government level: groups of new inhabitants had to be integrated into the receiving society and the social service system. This task not only posed financial and logistic questions but demanded structural reforms—and cooperation with societal actors. The following short overview of the socio-historical background in Germany and China exemplifies the challenges, differences and similarities with regard to migration in the two countries.

Starting with the end of the Second World War, Germany has seen four phases of immigratory flow: (1) The "re-settlers phase", when ethnic German expellees (*Vertriebene*) were forced to leave Central and Eastern Europe after 1945 and sought shelter in the then two separated halves of Germany, the Federal Republic of Germany and the German Democratic Republic. (2) The guest worker phase began in the 1950s. West Germany quickly began to recover with the economic support of the American Marshall Plan and workers were needed. Consequently, workers were invited from southern Europe, mainly from Italy in the 1950s, and from Spain, Greece, Turkey, Portugal and Yugoslavia in the 1960s. This time, integration was more of an issue, since the second generation of migrants came from a different language and cultural background than the first. Simultaneously, beginning in the 1950s, a second phase of ethnic German refugees (*Aussiedler*), again coming from Central and Eastern Europe, reached Germany. (3) The fall of the Wall in 1989 triggered migration to Germany among people with a German ethnic background who had lived in the Soviet Union. Against the background of the history of the Nazi regime and its crimes against humanity, which had triggered massive refugee migration, and in expectation of the returning ethnic German migrants, the Federal Republic of Germany instituted a broad right to seek asylum in its Constitution of 1949. This "open door policy" in Germany was not welcomed by all Germans and anti-foreigner sentiments rose in the 1980s and have become a more or less underlying problem in the context of immigration in Germany ever since. More recently, Germany's right of asylum was restricted considerably, while, on the other hand, the need for a foreign labour force was acknowledged by the Immigration Act, which came into force in 2005. However, in 2015, due to armed conflicts in the Middle East (Syria, Iraq, Afghanistan, etc.) and a very strict asylum policy in most European countries in the face of this challenge, in a fourth phase, an unprecedented number of almost 900,000 migrants entered Germany and presented a great challenge for the federal and particularly the local governments in Germany (Gluns 2017).

As for China, we understand domestic migration as referring to those people who move from one Chinese locality to another locality in China and change their residence for a longer period of time. As mentioned before, China experienced several phases of large migration as a consequence of the economic development in the PRC. These developments first took off in the affluent regions of China's east coast. Eastern China therefore functioned as a pull factor for labour migrants from poorer areas in central and western China. Apart from spatial problems of accommodating the large influx of people from poorer regions in the cities, the above-mentioned *hukou*-registration system posed a particular Chinese problem in the context of migration. Due to this system, the social security systems in rural and urban areas were separated. Earned entitlements could not be transferred from one place to another. Rural labour migrants and their families had no way of participating in urban social security systems. This meant that, at least in the initial years, they had no health insurance, no pension scheme, no unemployment insurance, and their children could not attend urban schools. These conditions remained in place even in more recent decades, when labour mobility was unofficially encouraged. Labour was increasingly in demand from the booming manufacturing and assembling industry in China, the "workbench of the world".

Therefore, as far as the integration of migrants is concerned, Germany and China face very different challenges. In Germany—the basic needs for food and shelter aside—the integration of immigrants is mostly a cultural, educational and language-related challenge. In addition, there is general anti-foreign sentiment in German society to contend with. For China, the biggest integration challenge for migrants is that into the social security system of their respective locality (Ma Xiulian 2017). In both cases, it is mainly the local government that bears the responsibility for successful integration. The next section expounds these administrative challenges and the role of societal actors in response to them.

The Role of Local Governments and Non-profit Organisations in Dealing With the Challenges of Migration

It is the local governments that bear the main burden of responsibility and work in dealing with the influx of migrants. This is due to the administrative organisations in Germany and China. In both countries, the local administration authorities are responsible for social service provision for the citizens and newly incoming migrants within their jurisdiction. And in both countries, local administration bodies have to act with limited budgets and under the urgent social pressure of the need to integrate the incoming people into the receiving communities.

In Germany, municipalities (*Kommunen*) represent the local government. According to the German constitution, a municipality is the lowest administrative level in the federal system. The so-called *principle of universality* purports that every task concerning a community is legally a municipal activity. The individual structure and capacities of the municipalities are defined in the communal constitutions of the federal states. Therefore, the size and form of the municipalities and also the communal power-sharing and suffrage systems vary slightly in the federal states. In general, the municipal council and the municipal administrative body are the basic spheres of local governance. The mayor, as head of municipal administration and chair of the municipal council, connects the two spheres. City-states such as Berlin have a slightly different structure because they are municipalities and federal states at the same time. Basically, local governments in Germany have the right of communal self-administration (Art. 28 II GG). According to this law, municipalities are able to administer and organise their matters and activities independently, unless federal or state law explicitly makes other arrangements. In the administrative hierarchy, roughly, the federal government is responsible for national issues, like foreign policy, defence, national infrastructures and financial administration, while the federal states are, among other things, responsible for education, the police and the courts. The municipalities, on the third and lowest administrative level in Germany, are responsible for the social and health sectors, public bodies and economic development. First and foremost, the municipalities execute most of the administrative activities. These administrative tasks on the municipal level include assigned tasks from upper administrative levels as well as tasks of self-administration, which again include obligatory and voluntary tasks. Tasks assigned to municipalities can constrain the manoeuvring space of these municipalities. The revenues of municipalities are composed of municipal tax revenues as well as vertical and horizontal fiscal compensation. The financing of assigned tasks is supposed to accompany each assignment from above. However, the assignment and also fiscal compensation constrain municipal decision-making power. In addition, the municipalities often complain that financial support is often not enough to fulfil additional tasks (Zimmer and Szeili 2017). The municipalities bear the largest part of the integration tasks along the current immigration phase, because many of the related policy areas are within the scope of their responsibilities. Against the backdrop of recent developments, the federal states and municipalities have successfully demanded additional federal means to cope with the additional tasks resulting from increased immigration. However, the municipalities still struggle to accomplish all the tasks due to tight finances and limited manpower (Gluns 2017).

In China, governance at the local level is decided and implemented by the local People's Congresses and the local governments which exist on the county, prefecture and provincial levels. Administrative responsibilities are also divided into central and local responsibilities. While the central government is responsible for national defence, diplomacy, security, boundaries, national strategic resources, prevention and control of national major infectious diseases, etc., the local governments take care of tasks such as social order, local traffic, public thoroughfares and community services. As for their expenditure, some have to follow national standards and are therefore shared proportionally between central and local governments, e.g. the expenditure on basic health insurance and compulsory education is borne to a large extent by the central government, while the expenditure on medical and health care as well as education is mainly borne by the local governments, with only a little portion taken on by the central government. Therefore, in China, local governments are under great pressure, too, as far as the fulfilment of their manifold tasks is concerned (Ma Qingyu et al. 2017).

This is why, in both countries, the governments have turned to nonprofit organisation (NPOs) for support, although their political systems and the governments' attitudes to NPOs differ greatly. The case studies in this research project show how the state and NPOs cooperate in providing services to migrants in four policy areas, namely education, employment, social services (including legal aid) and vulnerable groups.

We were interested in how the local administration coped with the challenges and how the relationship between the state and the NPOs unfolded in this area. From a historical perspective, we discovered interesting similarities between Germany and China which are worth a comparative approach. These similarities can be summarised as a corporatist tradition that has slowly made room for a neoliberal form of cooperation. The state's influence was pushed back in favour of those market forces that promised more efficient use and allocation of resources. Although these shifts took place in slightly different time periods in China and Germany, as the next section will show, in both countries there is a strong tendency towards a neoliberal approach of non-profit–government relations, i.e. considerations of cost-effectiveness and service provision are introduced into the formerly bureaucratic systems and lead, among other things, to the outsourcing of certain social services to external private providers.

State–NPO Relationships in Transition—Corporatism and Neoliberalism

One of the important observations made by the research project is that the relations between local governments and non-profit organisations have changed significantly in recent history, both in Germany and China. As this section will sketch out, research on the third sector[6] of both countries has identified (different variants of) corporatism as a framework that described the close relationship between the state and societal actors well until recently. As some of the contributions in this book discuss in more detail,[7] this characterisation has made way for other forms of relations such as marketised and network types of cooperation.

In the debate about China, corporatism is usually derived from Schmitter's idea of corporatism, i.e. a top-down conceptualisation of the relationship between the state and societal organisations in which "a limited number of singular, compulsory, noncompetitive, hierarchically ordered and functionally differentiated categories, recognized or licensed (if not created) by the state and granted a deliberate representational monopoly within their respective categories in exchange for observing certain controls on their selection of leaders and articulation of demands and supports" (Schmitter 1974, 93 f.). In other words, corporatism is mainly used to describe a particular hierarchical form of *interest representation* among societal organisations vis-à-vis the state. This view was deemed useful by scholars like Unger and Chan (1995) to grasp the role of state- or Chinese Communist Party (CCP)-initiated organisations (so-called government organised non-governmental organisations, GONGOs) which play an important role in the CCP conception of societal participation in party state governance. Similarly to imperial times, when the Chinese emperor's power would only reach down to a certain level of society, while grassroots society was governed by lower level administration bodies beyond the direct reach of the emperor, under the CCP the mass organisations were responsible for governing—and also listen to the grievances of—the grassroots level of society and for transforming this knowledge into policy. More sophisticated forms of corporatism were developed in later research literature. They are discussed in more detail in the contributions in this volume.

---

6 In this introduction and throughout the volume, we use third-sector to indicate the area of activity of non-profits which neither belongs to the state nor to the market.

7 See the contribution by Levy and Ketels and by Ma et al. in this volume.

For the description and explanation of the state–society relationship in European countries, particularly the German variant, a slightly different understanding of corporatism is applied which is not only concerned with *interest representation* but describes a *subsidiary form* of "governing society by formalized intersectoral and intermediary collaboration [...]" (Bode 2011, 117 f.).[8] In this sense, corporatist societies involve organised groups in rule-making and governing society. In the German case, this variant of governance is particular useful for understanding Germany's third sector, which, particularly in the welfare and social services domain, is organised in umbrella organisations, the German Welfare Associations and their affiliated members, which are organised independently and are not subject to state interference. At the same time, the Associations participate in rule-making processes concerning almost every welfare related policy area such as health or care for youngsters and children. The origins of this system date back to the German Empire, and it was consolidated in the Weimar Republic and—after a break during the Nazi period—re-established in the early years of the Federal Republic of Germany (Zimmer 1999, 40 f.).

In both countries, these corporatist forms of governance have been transformed and have made way for other forms of state–society relations, albeit at slightly different points in contemporary history. In China, societal organisations started to develop rapidly in the 1980s, following Deng Xiaoping's *Reform and Opening Policy*. While the Chinese third sector in the 1980s was still dominated by those organisations initiated by the state and/or the CCP, it started to diversify in the 1990s. Today, the GONGOs play a minor role in the third sector in China, and at least some societal sectors are now dominated by privately initiated organisations. This shift in the initiators of third sector organisations means that there is a large variety of actors, motivations and organisational goals, but it does not mean that Chinese NPOs can act completely independently today. They are still strictly controlled by a registration system that binds them closely to the state. In addition, they have to establish basic level CCP organisations inside their organisations as soon as they employ three or more CCP members.[9] To a large extent, NPOs in China are not membership-based[10] (influential exceptions are the state-run trade associations) and are therefore not

---

8 For more information on subsidiarity in Germany's third sector, see the contribution by Zimmer and Grabbe in this volume.
9 This is still the case under the recent legislation of the Charity Law and related legislation (Levy and Pissler 2020).
10 At the beginning of 2020, of the officially registered societal organisations in China 364,808 were membership-based associations and 487,011were organisations

primarily aimed at interest representation but rather focus on the provision of services. Another factor that is also part of the shift away from the corporatist system was the introduction of the government's procurement of services from third sector organisations. In our case studies, it becomes apparent that the highly competitive procedures of state procurement of services are greatly influenced by neoliberal considerations of efficiency and the reduction of costs. In short, roughly since the turn of the 21st century, the corporatist practice in China has slowly been transformed into a neoliberal, highly competitive system of government procurement of services from NPOs.

The German corporatist system's transformation had other causes. It was a system of subsidiarity, i.e. the firm establishment of the corporatist umbrella organisations, particularly in the areas of health and social services, in the 1960s, that actually transformed these organisations "into functional equivalents of public sector institutions" and that finally caused their dysfunctionality. In the early 1980s, they had seemingly turned into bureaucratic organisations that were as unresponsive as government institutions and, therefore, were unable to respond adequately to current societal trends. Accordingly, they had to face a significant loss of legitimacy. At the same time, neoliberal ideas had emerged since the 1970s and suggested that the rules of the free market could be the panacea to the so-called cost-disease of the German welfare state and particularly of health and social service provision. In the 1990s, the Welfare Associations, as the key providers of social services at that time, lost almost all their privileges; since then, they and their member organisations have had to compete with commercial enterprises when offering their services to local governments (Zimmer 1999).

In other words, the two countries find themselves in similar, post-corporatist periods of new orientation in state–NPO relations, China since the turn of the century, and Germany as early as since the 1980s. This astounding similarity[11] between the two countries, which otherwise are so different as regards their history, culture, size, population density, economic development, political system and so on, encouraged us to set up a research design that included field research in both countries and a comparative perspective. This research design will be presented in the next section.

---

without members (479,375 social services organisations and 7,636) foundations) (Source: http://data.chinanpo.gov.cn/, last access: 23 January 2020).

11 Actually, we found even more similarities; see the contributions by Levy and Ketels and Ma, Xie and Li.

Katja Levy, Annette Zimmer, Qingyu Ma

Methodology of the Research Project and a Typology of State–NPO Relations

The LoGoSO project is a research project encompassing three research teams. The basic division of work of the research teams was that one German team was responsible for the fieldwork in Germany and one Chinese team was responsible for the field research in China. A further German team served as the coordination hub, was responsible for the organisational and administrative management of the project and ensuring the comparability of the data collected and compliance with scientific quality standards, and it conducted comparative research.

Field research was conducted in two cities in each country. We selected Berlin and Guangzhou as two of the largest cities in their countries. Cologne and Hangzhou represent two medium-sized cities that function as economic hubs in their region. All four cities are immigrant cities with a well-established third sector.[12] The nineteen cases of local government–NPO cooperation that form the core of the study were selected from four policy areas: education, employment, social assistance (including legal aid) and vulnerable groups. We chose these policy areas with the goal of ensuring comparability and researchability. Policy areas were chosen (1) that were significant in the pursuit of integrating the different types of migrants in the receiving communities in China and Germany; (2) that involved equal cooperation between the state and NPOs (instead of being dominated by one of them) in both countries; and (3) that were equally accessible to the researchers in both countries. Preliminary desktop research on the services offered by NPOs to migrants in the two countries revealed that the above-mentioned four policy areas fulfil these criteria.[13] The selected cases were cooperative projects or programmes by NPOs and local gov-

---

12 See Ketels 2019 for more details on the case cities. Beijing was an early choice as a sample city. The idea was to include two capital cities in the study, Berlin and Beijing. However, in 2017, in the course of the research project, the Beijing government decided to cap its population and send home a significant proportion of its migrant population (see Hornby 2017). In this situation, research on the integration of the migrant population in Beijing would have met serious obstacles. Therefore, Guangzhou was selected instead. This city is characterised by a significant need for migrant integration due to the large production capacities of the city with their insatiable need for rural migrant workers.

13 In the selection of the policy areas, we had to take into account that the two countries differ with regard to the service areas for migrants that are usually supported by NPOs and those that are solely provided by the governments. For example, housing, is an important service offered to migrants by NPOs in Germany, but it is not a typical service offered by NPOs in China. Health was also excluded as a

ernments focusing on service provision for migrants in these policy areas, and they were selected to vary with respect to NPO size, age (year of establishment), migrant involvement in operations, funding source, competition and administrative level.

Moreover, each group was supposed to identify and analyse one unsuccessful case, i.e. a case in which the cooperation with local government failed. These "failed cases" were added in order to cross-check the results on the conditions that lead to the success or failure of cooperation.[14] Another complex aspect of ensuring comparability was to control the typology of organisations. The researchers had to make sure that they were referring to similar types of organisations. The core problem in this respect was the fact that the two countries have very different approaches concerning the organisational definitions of NPOs. The first difference is that in Germany it is not the organisational form that indicates whether an NPO is a charitable organisation or a for-profit enterprise, but it is the tax authority which makes the final judgement in this matter. A limited liability company can be a non-profit in Germany if it does not distribute its profits to its owners/shareholders, but reinvests a considerable share of them into the charitable goal of the organisation. On the other hand, a German foundation could be regarded as a for-profit organisation by the tax authorities if its purpose is not charitable, for example a family foundation whose purpose to generate a regular income for family members only. In contrast, in China, organisations have to register in one of three organisational forms, i.e. a foundation, social service organisation or association. These organisational forms are, by legal definition, non-profits. More recently, the Charity Law (2016) has opened up new ways for Chinese NPOs to solicit donations if they register, in addition to their NPO status, as *charity* organisations.[15]

All in all, 71 interviews were conducted in Germany and China between July 2018 and April 2019. The German and Chinese research teams

---

service area in the investigation because the organisational structure of the health systems in China and Germany proved to be too different to be comparable.

14 As anticipated, it turned out to be very difficult to find "failed cases". However, the project teams managed to find three cases, one each in Guangzhou, Berlin and Hangzhou, but did not succeed in finding one in Cologne. Therefore, the total number of cases is nineteen, not twenty. See Tables 3 and 4 in the appendix of the chapter by Levy and Ketels.

15 See Levy and Pissler 2020 on the details and implication of the new legislation in China. See Tables 3 and 4 in the appendix of the chapter by Levy and Ketels for the organisational forms of the case organisations.

adopted a "general field guide" developed by the coordinating team that was used as a guideline or masterplan for the empirical research conducted in Germany and China and which was adapted when necessary. In this way, it was ensured that across the countries, policy areas and different actor constellations the data collected was indeed comparable and suitable for comparative analysis afterwards. Interviewees in both countries comprised of managers, staff and volunteers of the NPOs as well as local government representatives. Backed by desktop research and observations, the interviews lay the foundation for the in-depth case studies.[16]

The contributions in this volume present part of the results of the LoGoSO project against the background of the societal developments and challenges described above and based on the methodology and theoretical framework presented.

The Contributions in this Volume

In her contemporary portrait of the third sector in Germany, Annette Zimmer looks at the traditional background, legal framework, and recent changes to the cooperation relationship between the state and NPOs. In her analysis, she points out that it might be advisable to introduce a legal form for non-profits, although this would be a radical novelty in the third sector of the country.

Zimmer and Grabbe's article focuses on Germany and gives an overview of the different traditions and models of public administration. In particular, the authors explicate the German "dual system" of social service provision that is characterised by a link between local self-government and subsidiary social services provision. Recent shifts in the history of German public administration had a profound impact on the relations between the local governments and the service providing NPOs. The former very privileged NPOs have to compete with a multitude of other actors for government subsidies. The findings of this paper present the backdrop to the German cases of the research project.

Lovelady and Grabbe analyse the German cases of the project's sample with special attention to the modes of cooperation between local governments and NPOs from a public administration perspective. They find that

---

16 The primary reports on the public administration traditions in the cities and selected case reports are in the process of being published in Chinese with the National Academy of Governance Press (国家行政管理出版社出版).

in the sample cases "third-party government" and "network governance" were the preferred modes of cooperation. While "third-party government" describes a mode of cooperation in which a non-profit organisation closely cooperates in a quite formalised and at arm's length way with the local government, "network governance" was orchestrated by the local government in two German cases and in one case by the NPO with the aim of facilitating the exchange of knowledge and cooperation among the non-profits in charge as well as among different units of governments and non-profits. "Third-party government" was strongly pushed forward by the sudden increase in incoming migrants beginning in 2015 and the consequential increase in service demand. At the same time, the local governments turned to "network governance" in order to improve service efficiency and information flow. However, except for employment, which is a federal responsibility in Germany, the service cooperation in the other fields varied immensely in the different German cities. This study supports Zimmer and Grabbe's argument that the old German system of subsidiarity is in the process of dissolution. Service providing organisations are no longer necessarily closely linked to umbrellas, in particular to the Welfare Associations.

Levy and Ketels take a comparative point of view and compare the modes of cooperation in China and Germany. They find that outsourcing, particularly in the form described by Salamon (1987) as third-party government, is put into practice in both countries. Networking is another trait that they find evidence of in all the organisations. However, in contrast to Lovelady and Grabbe, who find networking in two of the three networks as a top-down feature of the local governments in Germany, Levy and Ketels take a bottom-up perspective on networking and find that all organisations practise networking for a range of reasons. These perhaps surprising similarities between the state–NPO modes of cooperation in Germany and China stand in sharp contrast to the differences in rationales that Levy and Ketels also point out in their article.

Ketels and Levy adapt Jennifer Coston's model of government–NPO relationships to accommodate the cases of both Germany and China. They find that the original model is very helpful for categorising such relationships in Western countries, but that they do not capture the situation in China correctly. The two authors propose an adaptation of Coston's model that is applicable to NPO–state relationships in Western liberal democracies and the PRC, but may also be applicable to other countries with widely varying regimes.

Ma, Xie and Li make an overall comparative assessment of local governments' relationships with NPOs in Germany and China through the lens of corporatism as defined by Schmitter (1974) and Streeck/Kenworthy (2005). They find that the differences between local state–NPO cooperation in China and Germany can be categorised into legal framework, registration conditions, supervision, cooperation balance and the delimitation between the state and NPOs. They then compare the nature of state–NPO relations in the two countries with eleven indicators based on Schmitter (Schmitter, 1974). Their results show that corporatism is very different in practice in Germany and China. It is inclined towards national corporatism in China, while in Germany towards social corporatism with a weakening tendency. Different types of corporatism lead to different state–NPO relations, thus affecting the trend of citizen association and the effect of NPOs participating in social services. This experience is of profound inspiration to both countries.

In the conclusion, Lovelady and Ketels summarise the overall results of this book and the research project.

References

Bode, Ingo (2011). Creeping Marketization and Post-corporatist Governance: The Transformation of State-nonprofit Relations in Continental Europe. In: Phillips, Susan D./ Rathgeb Smith, Steven (eds.) *Governance and Regulation in the Third Sector: International Perspectives*. Florence/KY: Routledge, 115–141.

Coston, Jennifer M. (1998). "A Model and Typology of Government-NGO Relationships", *Non-profit and Voluntary Sector Quarterly*, 27:3, 358–382.

Gluns, Danielle (2017). Report 4 "Current Migration Trends in Germany". Available online at: https://logosoprojectsite.files.wordpress.com/2017/02/t4-current-migration-trends-in-germany.pdf (last access: 17 January 2020).

Hornby, Lucy (2017). Beijing's migrants no longer welcome as city caps population. China's capital to introduce 23m limit and shrink footprint by tearing down buildings. The Financial Times (20 April 2017). Available online at: https://www.ft.com/content/822e982c-1b40-11e7-bcac-6d03d067f81f (last access: 5 May 2020).

Ketels, Anja (2019). "Migrant Integration as a Challenge for Local Governments and Social Organizations in China and Germany – Policy Traditions and Integration Measures in Guangzhou, Hangzhou, Berlin and Cologne", *LoGoSO Research Papers Nr. 8*. Available online at: https://refubium.fu-berlin.de/handle/fub188/24154.

Levy, Katja and Knut Benjamin Pissler (2020). *Charity with Chinese Characteristics. Chinese Charitable Foundations between the Party-state and Society*. Cheltenham: Edward Elgar.

Ma Qingyu and Jida Fan, Miaomiao Shan (2017). Report 1. "Reform and Development of the Regional Public Administration System in China" (unpublished).

Ma, Xiulian (2017). Report 3 "Migration Trends and Challenges in China" (unpublished).

Unger, Jonathan and Anita Chan (1995). "China, Corporatism, and the East Asian Model", *The Australian Journal of Chinese Affairs*, 33 (January), 29–53.

Salamon, Lester (1987). Of Market Failure, Voluntary Failure, and Third-Party Government: toward a Theory of Government–Nonprofit Relations in the Modern Welfare State, *Nonprofit and Voluntary Sector Quarterly*, 16:1–2, 29–49.

Schmitter, Philippe C. (1974). "Still the Century of Corporatism?" *The Review of Politics*, 36:1, 85–131.

Streeck, Wolfgang and Lane Kenworthy (2005). "Theories and practices of neocorporatism." In Thomas Janoski, Robert R. Alford, Alexander M. Hicks and M. A. Schwartz (eds.), *The Handbook of Political Sociology: States, Civil Societies, and Globalization*. Cambridge: Cambridge University Press, 441–460.

Zimmer, Annette (1999). "Corporatism Revisited – The Legacy of History and the German Nonprofit-Sector", *Voluntas*, 10:1, 37–49.

Zimmer, Annette and Judith Szeili (2017). Report 2 "Local Public Administration and Governance in Comparative Perspective". Available online at: https://logosoprojectsite.files.wordpress.com/2017/02/t2-local-government-andadministration.pdf, last access: 17 January 2020.

Germany's Non-profit Sector—from Growth to its Limits?

Annette Zimmer

1. Introduction

Close cooperation with government has been the hallmark of the German non-profit sector since the late 19th century. In contrast to Anglo-Saxon countries, German non-profits have never perceived themselves per se as a "countervailing power" vis-à-vis the state. Instead, government–non-profit relationships have been traditionally based on a model of partnership and reciprocity. However, this model is no longer strongly in place. Today, the sector perceives itself as being in a state of flux and confronted with a significantly changed environment. Government support has become unstable und financially insufficient. As a consequence, non-profits are increasingly turning to the market. There are still many small non-profits in local communities, operating exclusively with volunteers. However, particularly in the social domain, non-profits are highly professionalised and increasingly business-like, since they have to compete with a growing number of for-profit competitors. In addition, the legal framework does not provide a supportive environment for the business activities of German non-profits. The purpose of this article is to provide a portrait of the German non-profit sector by highlighting its traditional embeddedness, outlining the legal framework of German non-profits and addressing the question of whether the success story of the sector might be from growth to its limits.

2. Germany's Subsidiary Model of Non-profit–Government Relationships

2.1 Distinctive Models of Government–Non-profit Relationships

Comparative studies on non-profit government relationships (Salamon et al. 1999; Zimmer/Priller 2007) identified three distinctive patterns of non-profit–government relationships: the "liberal", the "social democratic" and "subsidiary" models. Germany used to be strongly in line with the subsidiary model. However, nowadays the country is increasingly moving towards the liberal model. With a special focus on the German non-profit sector, the three models will be briefly portrayed.

Table 1: Models of Non-profit–Government Relationships

Model	Liberal	Social Democratic	Subsidiary
Input Side Relevance of NPOs	High voice, lobbying	High voice	Low incorporated
Output Side Relevance of NPOs	High integrated in a market-economy-based way	Low barely any service provision	High incorporated into the welfare state
Outreach	Anglo-Saxon countries	Scandinavia	Central Europe

Source: Freise/Zimmer 2004: 163 updated

The *liberal model* translates into a situation in which non-profit organisations hold an important control function as regards the government and its administrative apparatus. In addition, and against the background of a rudimentary welfare state, non-profits play an important role as social service providers. As such, they compete with private companies engaged in social service provision. In the social domain, cooperation between non-profits and the government is organised in accordance with the rules of the market and based on contracts. In a very competitive environment, the non-profits have to be efficiently managed and are therefore predominantly run by professionals. The countries that traditionally represent this model are the Anglo-Saxon countries, especially the United States.

The *social democratic model* is closely connected with the growth of the labour movement and the development of the welfare state. Social democratic parties, labour unions and a broad spectrum of voluntary organisations, such as sports and cultural clubs, constitute the backbone of this model. In the social democratic model, non-profits are not highly engaged in social service provision. Providing the infrastructure for leisure activities as well as giving citizens a voice to express and to channel their ideas into the government's apparatus via trade unions or other encompassing societal organisations constitute the key functions of non-profits in the social democratic model of non-profit–government relationships that is strongly in place in Scandinavian countries.

The *subsidiary model* is linked with "the principle of subsidiarity" of 19th century Catholic ethics. In essence, government has to remain uninvolved as long as "the smaller decentralised unit" is sufficiently capable of handling affairs independently. However, the government is, by the same token, obliged to provide a "helping hand" as soon as "the smaller unit"—be it a citizen or a non-profit organisation—is in need of protection and financial support. In contrast to the liberal model, a rigid division between the state and society is not at the core of the subsidiary model. On the contrary, the government is highly inclined to work with non-profit organisations. In addition, non-profit social service provision is thoroughly integrated into the welfare state and protected from commercial competition. In contrast to the social democratic model, the voice function of non-profits is not appreciated by the government. Instead, non-profits, in particular at the local level, are perceived as vehicles for societal integration. They provide a "homeland" for their members; as transmitters of norms and values, non-profits guarantee societal stability and harmony. The subsidiary model used to be most strongly in place in Central European countries and particularly in Germany, which until very recently provided a textbook example of this particular model of government–non-profit relationships (Anheier/Seibel 2001).

2.2 Current Changes in German Non-profit–Government Relationships

In Germany, the close cooperation between non-profits and the government, tailored in accordance with the subsidiary model, was an outcome of the country's troublesome history. In the time of the German Empire, the country's society was very heterogeneous and divided into strong societal cleavages and milieus, of which the social democratic and the Catholic, representing the left, and the conservative right of the political spectrum were the most prominent ones. The left and the right camp of German society were populated and glued together by numerous non-profit organisations and voluntary associations, which were active in a broad spectrum of activities, stretching from social service provision to sports and leisure. Alongside the development of the welfare state, German governments at the local and federal levels took advantage of non-profit organisations. In particular, non-profits served as vehicles for alleviating conflicts between the different milieus. Also, the German government built on the pioneering role of non-profits in many areas of social service provision. The principle of subsidiarity served as a normative underpinning of the cooperation (Zimmer 2004).

Up until the early 1990s, the principle safeguarded that, in central areas of social service provision such as health, care for the elderly or child-care, non-profit organisations were not only legally protected from commercial competition but also enjoyed secure government funding. However, over the past few decades and in accordance with the growing importance of neo-liberal thinking, the government has dismantled the once privileged position of non-profit organisations. Today, as regards the provision of so-cial services, the organisational or legal form of the provider no longer matters. Particularly in the social domain, non-profits work in highly com-petitive markets, where they have to compete for government contracts with for-profit commercial providers (Zimmer/Paul 2018). Against this background, it is argued that, similarly to other countries, the German government should introduce a special legal form for non-profits that are engaged in service provision (Zimmer/Priller 2019). However, up until now the legal and organisational forms introduced and partly earmarked for non-profit activity in the second half of the 19th century are still in place.

3. The Legal Environment of German Non-profit Organisations

3.1 Legal Stipulations and Organisational Forms

The German approach to regulating non-profit activities combines the tra-dition of a civil law country expressing a high degree of government con-trol with the concept of self-governance. Non-profit activity and self-gover-nance of citizens are welcomed and protected by law; however, govern-ment via registration procedures and explicit regulation closely defines the purposes, functions and activities of non-profit organisations. Unanimous-ly, the legal stipulations earmarked for non-profit activities were first codi-fied in the German Empire's Civil Law Code (*Bürgerliches Gesetzbuch*) of 1870/72. Albeit modified to a certain extent, these legal stipulations are still in place. The most important and widely used legal forms for organis-ing non-profit activities are:

- registered association (*eingetragener Verein*),
- cooperative (*Genossenschaft*),
- private limited company (*GmbH*), and
- private law foundation (*Stiftung des Privatrechts*).

Drawing on both the distinction between member-based and non-mem-ber-based organisations and on the divide between commercial and non-commercial activities, the categorisation of the aforementioned organisa-tional forms translates into the following typology:

Table 2: Typology of Legal Forms for Organising NPO Activities

	Member-based	Non-member-based
Non-commercial	Registered Association *Eingetragener Verein*	Private Law Foundation *Stiftung des Privatrechts*
Commercial	Cooperative *Genossenschaft*	Private Limited Company *Gemeinschaft mit beschränkter Haftung*

Source: Zimmer et al 2004: 690

Registered Association/Eingetragener Verein

A registered association is designed as a member-based organisation expressing a high degree of reciprocity. It is defined as a voluntary alliance of at least seven individual or legal persons who jointly want to accomplish a certain goal or purpose. The association becomes a legal entity via registration in the Association Register (*Vereinsregister*) maintained locally at county courts (*Amtsgerichte*). In order to be eligible for registration, associations must pursue non-commercial activities and must qualify for public benefit status (*Gemeinnützigkeit*). In the past, registration procedures opened the doors to rigid governmental supervision. Today, government authorities interpret the registration requirements liberally. Designed as a membership organisation, there is no capital requirement to start a *Verein*. The association is not obliged to publish its accounts. Liability is limited to its assets. With respect to internal governance, *Vereine* enjoy the freedom to establish any kind of advisory boards or other organisational sub-units. Due to its flexible governance structure, limited liability and relatively easy foundation procedures, the *Verein* has developed into the most popular vehicle for organising non-profit activities in Germany.

Cooperative/Genossenschaft

Cooperatives aim at enhancing the economic well-being of their members. In Germany, social entrepreneurs originally founded cooperatives with the goal of promoting an economy based on solidarity (Zimmer/Priller 2019). Cooperatives still play a significant role in Germany's economy. However, the majority of them perceive themselves as an integral part of Germany's market economy and no longer qualify for public benefit status. In recent years, however, the notion of solidarity as an important aspect of cooperatives has been rediscovered. Many so-called social cooperatives have recently been founded in the areas of housing, in particular for the elderly (*Seniorengenossenschaften*), or in the field of energy production (*Energiegenossenschaften*) (Zimmer/Priller 2019).

Private Law Foundation/Stiftung des Privatrechts

According to German law, foundations are legal entities based on an endowment. While federal law regulates some aspects of foundation activities, the registration, approval and supervision of foundations are a matter of the regional governments, the German *Länder*. In line with this, the establishment of a foundation requires the consent of the respective government authority (*Stiftungsbehörde*), which issues the approval based on a concessionary system whereby the state government grants the foundation the right to establish itself for a set of purposes which must be in accordance with the requirements codified for attaining public benefit status. The liability of a foundation is limited to the extent of its assets. With respect to internal governance, foundations are very similar to associations and are quite flexible regarding their organisational structures and governance. They are only obliged to report on their activities to the local tax authority yearly. There is no further legal requirement such as publishing an annual report.

Private Limited Company/Gemeinschaft mit beschränkter Haftung

The private limited company (*GmbH*) is regulated by commercial law and primarily designed for organising business activities. The company is a corporation of members based on capital (minimum 25,000 euros) or shares. The company is a legal person facing only minimal registration requirements and limited public oversight. Attaining legal capacity is linked to registration at the federal Register of Companies; the company may be established for any lawful purpose as certified by a public notary. In order to be awarded tax-exempt status, thus qualifying as a non-profit organisation, a *GmbH* must pursue non-commercial activities and act in accordance with the requirements linked to public benefit status. Apart from official financial monitoring for taxation purposes, there is no state supervision of limited companies.

With the exception of the private law foundation, which is designed by law to act on behalf of the furtherance of the public good none of these organisational forms is non-commercial as such. Cooperatives and private limited companies are commercial in the sense that they further the business interests of their members or stareholders. If they fulfil special requirements laid out in tax law, they are awarded public benefit status. Voluntary associations (*Vereine*) become vehicles for organising non-profit activities if they qualify for registration (*chartered association or eingetragener Verein. e.V.*). In sum, it is the German fiscal code that predominantly shapes the regulatory environment of the German non-profit sector.

3.2 Tax Laws and Tax Incentives

In Germany, qualifying for tax exemption or tax preferences is closely linked to tax regulations that specify the requirements organisations have to fulfil in order to be eligible for such privileges. Tax exemption is granted if an organisation's activities and purposes are in line with the regulations of the German Fiscal Code (*Abgabenordnung*). The Code provides a detailed list of organisational functions and purposes that qualify for tax exemption and tax preferences (Anheier/Seibel 2001: 17). Compliance with these requirements is checked by the local revenue service, which is also responsible for awarding tax privileges. While tax exemption (income and property tax and VAT) is related to the organisation, tax preferences are linked to donations made by individuals and corporations.

Income tax regulations serve as an indicator with which to assess how closely non-profits are allowed to engage in business activities. In Germany, there is a comparatively strict divide between the non-profit and for-profit sectors. While income derived from activities in furtherance of a non-profit purpose is tax exempt, "unrelated business income" enjoys tax-exempt status only up to the limit of about €30,000, which is far too low to be considered an important source of revenue. Under certain circumstances, there is the possibility of an organisation qualifying for tax exemption if it meets specific requirements that declare the business activities as being related to the organisation's purpose (*Zweckbetrieb*). The dividing line is sometimes very difficult to draw. Congruent with its civil law tradition, German legislation tends to formulate extensive catalogues of special cases for tax exemption, with the effect that tax regulations have become very complicated.

With respect to tax preferences, German law favours income tax deductions which reduce the amount of income subject to taxation, thus providing an incentive for wealthy donors. For good reasons, there are limits to deductibility. However, again there is no general rule. How much a donor might deduct from his or her taxable income depends on an organisation's purpose, activity and legal form. For example, donations to foundations enjoy more favourable deductibility treatment than those to voluntary associations (*Vereine*). As a general rule, membership dues are not considered eligible for deduction. Again, however, there is an extensive catalogue of exceptions (e.g., party membership dues are tax exempt), which turns German tax law into a puzzling subject. Not surprisingly, complexity and a lack of transparency are central topics of tax law criticism in Germany.

4. The Success Story of Germany's Non-profit Sector from Growth to its Limits?

Despite the country's rather complicated legal environment, the German non-profit sector can look back upon a remarkable success story since the mid 1970s. From a quantitative point of view, the registered association (*eingetragener Verein*) is the most important and frequently used legal form for organising non-profit activities in Germany. Currently, there are more than 600,000 registered associations operating in a variety of areas in the country (Krimmer 2019: 5).

Figure 1: Number of Registered Associations, 1960–2018

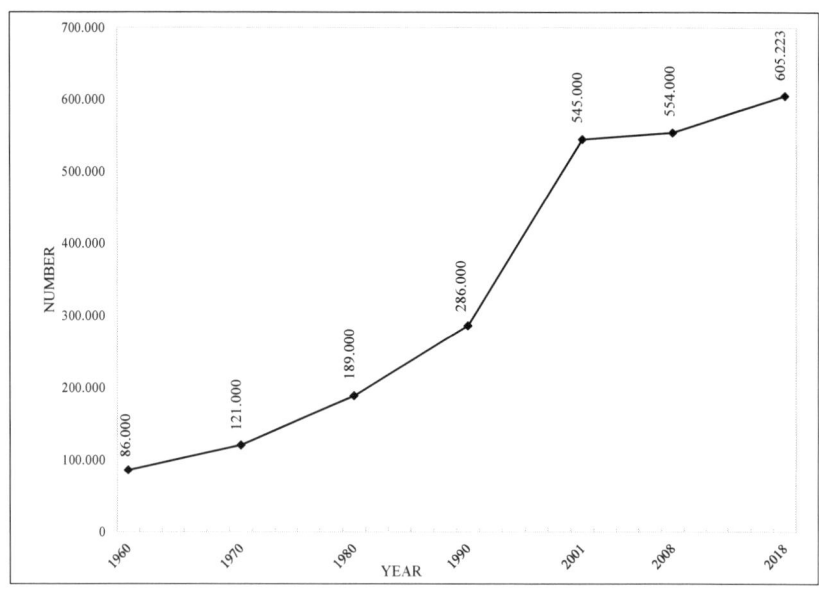

Source: Krimmer 2021 (Datenreport: forthcoming)

The majority of these associations are small or medium-sized; they are predominately active locally and manage their operations primarily with volunteer-input at the management and shop-floor levels. In the area of recreation and sports alone, there are around 90,000 sport clubs all over Germany (Priemer et al 2019: 33). There are fluctuations in the numbers of associations that are founded yearly, but all in all the number of voluntary associations is quite stable and is increasing steadily.

The backbone of Germany's registered associations are their volunteers, who run the organisations at the levels of management and service provision. Every five years, the German Federal Government in cooperation with private foundations conducts a "survey on volunteering" in which more than 20,000 Germans take part. The survey was put in place in the aftermath of the Commission of the Federal Parliament for the Study of Civic Engagement (Enquete-Kommission 2002). The results of the most recent survey on volunteering show that about 40 per cent of the German population volunteer on a regular basis (Simonson et al. 2017: 22; Kausmann et al. 2019: 56). With respect to the areas of volunteer engagement, sports and recreation constitutes the most popular area of volunteer activity. The data highlight schools and kindergartens as the second most important area of volunteering in Germany. The popularity of this field of activity is a very recent development since schooling and partly also child-rearing are perceived as prime responsibilities of the welfare state. Due to financial difficulties in local communities, many schools and partly also kindergartens are not in good condition in Germany. Private initiatives are implemented to make up for insufficient government support in terms of building upkeep or additional programmes such as field trips, visit to museums, etc.

Figure 2: Areas of Preference for Volunteer Activity: Engagement in Percentages

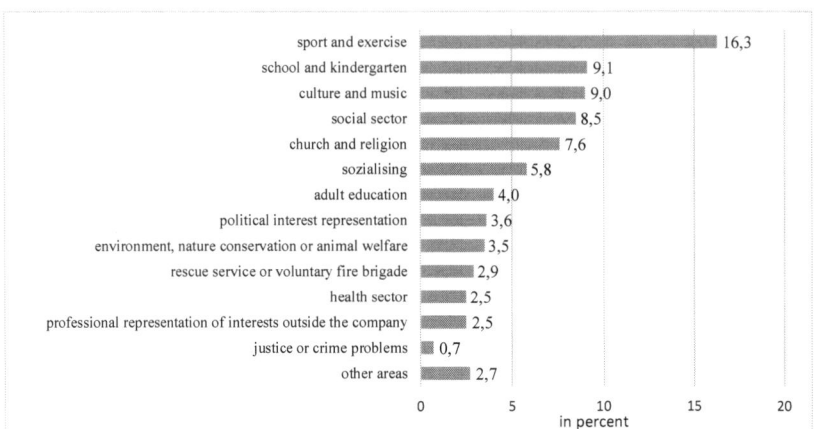

Source: https://www.bmfsfj.de/blob/113702/53d7fdc57ed97e4124fffec0ef5562a1/
vierter-freiwilligensurvey-monitor-data.pdf

Compared to voluntary associations, the development of foundations has been less stable during the last few decades. Traditionally, Germany used to be a country of foundations. However, the turbulent history of the country resulted in a significant downturn in the number of foundations after the First and Second World Wars. Moreover, it was impossible to set up a foundation in the former Democratic Republic of Germany (GDR) in the eastern part of the country. As clearly documented by the data, foundations have become increasingly popular since the 1990s. In addition, their founding peaked when the German government facilitated the setting-up of foundations. By now, there are around 22,000 active foundations in the country (Priemer et al. 2019: 36). However, founding a foundation has become less popular in recent years, the overall annual rate having slowed down since the mid 2000s for several reasons. Firstly, very low interest rates have made it difficult to invest foundation assets safely and profitably. Also, the foundation hype that was triggered by new government regulations has been watered down. Finally, it became clear that the majority of foundations are far too small in terms of their assets to have a societal impact.

Figure 3: New Foundations in Germany 1990–2018

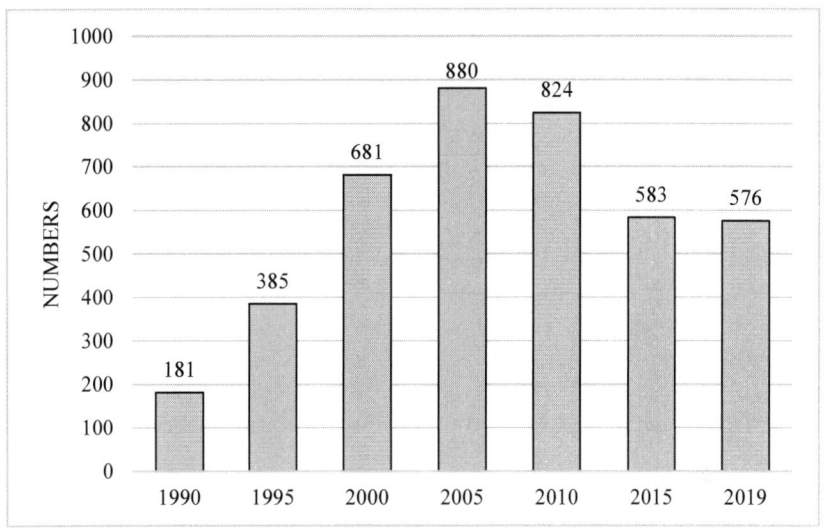

Source: Krimmer 2021 (Datenreport: forthcoming)

The majority of German foundations are small and middle-sized organisations; however, there are also a few very large operating foundations such as the Robert Bosch, Bertelsmann or Mercator Foundation. These foundations are corporate foundations in the sense that they are thoroughly or partly the owners and hence also the beneficiaries of the profits of each respective company. Through their programmes and working as think tanks, the foundations hold a prominent position in public discourse. In addition, these foundations work closely together with selected ministries of the German federal government with the aim of advancing specific projects or topics. Textbook examples of the cooperation between the "world of foundations" and the federal government are the campaigns on behalf of the dissemination of the concept of community foundations or the campaign for fostering corporate social responsibility. The cooperation between foundations and the government comprises joint funding of projects and common public campaigns.

Compared to registered associations and foundations, there are fewer non-profit cooperatives in Germany (Zimmer/Priller 2019, Primer et al. 2019: 10). However, some of the more recently founded cooperatives are working in interesting areas, such as solar power or wind energy (Zimmer/Priller 2019).

Finally, there is a growing number of non-profits organised as limited liability companies with tax-exempt status (Priller et al. 2012). According to the Datenreport (Primer et al. 2019: 10), particularly in recent years, the number of tax-exempt limited liability companies (*gGmbHs*) has been increasing steadily (from 17,300 in 2010 to 25,300 in 2016). These non-profits operate predominantly in the social domain providing healthcare or social services. The reason why this legal form is preferred by non-profits operating in these areas is closely linked with the recent changes in government policies. Instead of cooperating exclusively with non-profits, the government decided to partly replace the principle of subsidiarity by introducing the logic of competitive markets in the social domain. In addition, for-profit social service and healthcare providers became eligible to operate in these newly created markets, where they compete with non-profits for government contracts and social insurance allowances. Since non-profits no longer enjoy a preferential status as social service providers, they have tried to adapt themselves to the new environment by becoming similar to their competitors, the private companies operating in the welfare area. Accordingly, the non-profits in the social domain increasingly change their organisational form by opting to become limited liability companies with tax-exempt status, which puts them closer to the corporate sector. The reason why this shift towards the corporate sector is important and impacts significantly on the sector at large is linked to the fact that non-profit employment is heavily concentrated in this segment of Germany's non-profit sector.

The sector's share of total employment amounts to nine per cent, and it accounts for about four per cent of the country's GDP (Zimmer et al. 2013: 23). However, the non-profits that are active in the social domain, where they are working on par with both for-profit and government social service providers, are the strongholds of non-profit employment in Germany. Almost two million people, which equals about 70 per cent of the non-profit workforce, are employed by the membership organisations of the German Welfare Associations, which are the nationwide umbrellas of the non-profits operating in the social domain (Boeßenecker/Vilain 2013).

Table 3: Number of Facilities and Employees of the German Welfare Associations, 2018

Type or Focus of Assistance	Institutions	Full-time Employees	Part-time Employees
Healthcare	7,763	2,235,453	178,039
Youth	41,884	173,175	245,764
Family	4,787	6,207	18,614
Senior citizens	19,515	146,230	362,528
People with disabilities	19,071	162,315	220,555
People in special social situations	10,486	19,766	24,866
Others	13,426	47,058	43,604
Basic, non-basic, and continuous training for people in social and healthcare occupations	1,691	14,589	13,901
Total	118,623	804,795	1,107,870

Source: Bundesarbeitsgemeinschaft der Freien Wohlfahrtspflege (2018). Gesamtstatistik, Berlin: 7: https://www.bagfw.de/fileadmin/user_upload/V eroeffentlichungen/Publikationen/Statistik/BAGFW_Gesamtstatistik_2016 .pdf.

Although these numbers are impressive, the market share of non-profits in selected segments of the social service and healthcare economy has been shrinking since the principle of subsidiarity was watered down and the government opened up the market of social services to for-profit commercial providers in the 1990s. A case in point is the healthcare industry and particularly hospitals that were exclusively operated by either non-profits or local and regional governments. Since the early 1990s, when the government invited for-profit providers to enter this market, their market share has increased steadily, while the number of public hospitals has decreased significantly and the share of non-profit hospitls slightly. Even more acute is the situation in the area of home care for the elderly. Public service provision is almost non-existent; non-profit providers hold about a third of the market, while for-profit organisations are the market leaders with a share of about 65 per cent (Zimmer/Paul 2018: 106). These figures might be first indicators of a development towards growth to the limits of the German non-profit sector, whose economic strength and importance as a part of the labour market is based on its integration into the country's welfare state. In addition, the downturn of the economy might also lead to a slowing down of newly founded voluntary associations (*Vereine*) and foundations (*Stiftungen*) that are founded. At least, the most recent data already indicate a trend in this direction. All in all, the German non-profit sector, which used to operate very closely to the state, might be in need of change in order to reposition itself closer to the market.

5. In Need of Change!

The German non-profit sector used to operate in an organisational niche where organisations were secure from commercial competition thanks to the principle of subsidiarity and supported by the government from the local up to the national level of governance. Due to government protection, the organisations were not forced to act in a business-like manner. On the contrary, their legal and organisational forms, which were set in place by the government, kept them away from the commercial sector. The most common legal form of non-profits in Germany especially, the registered association, is not well equipped for business activities. However, over the past few decades and in accordance with the growing importance of neoliberal thinking, the government has gradually dismantled the once privileged position of non-profit organisations. The niche for non-profit activities has become narrower and far less government protected. At the same time, however, non-profits in Germany face significant difficulties from a legal perspective when they try to be competitive and business-like with the goal of becoming financially more sustainable. Against this background, it might be advisable to rethink the strict divide between the commercial for-profit and the community-oriented non-profit sector. It might be worthwhile considering the potential of the non-profit sector as a seedbed of a new solidarity economy. As an important step this might include reconsidering the legal framework of non-profit activity in Germany.

Current tax regulations are not in compliance with modern finance management. In Germany, tax-exempt NPOs are bound to disburse financial resources for statutory purposes in a timely manner, which means presently, consecutively and continuously (§§ 55–58 *Abgabenordnung*, General Tax Statute). Thus, without jeopardising the tax-privileged status of an organisation, German tax law does not allow for the accumulation of earnings over time. It is evident that the combined rules of non-distribution, timely disbursement, accumulation as well as expenditure restrictions seriously impede credit financing and therefore pose significant obstacles to modern financial management. In sum, the regulatory environment of German non-profit organisations is in need of change, which will require:

simplifying the catalogue of goals and purposes that qualify an organisation for public benefit status, modifying those legal stipulations that restrict non-profits from engaging even in those business activities that are related to their core purpose and activity,

developing a legal form that allows non-profits to engage in business activities without jeopardising their tax-exempt status.

Up until now it has been unclear in which direction non-profit organisations are developing. The German government is still very reluctant to initiate significant reforms as regards the legal stipulations for non-profit activity. In particular, it is very unlikely that in the near future German lawmaking will put forward a specific legal form, indeed a non-profit or social enterprise, that enjoys tax-exempt status, while simultaneously allowing entrepreneurial activities on competitive markets.

References

Anheier, Helmut K. and Wolfgang Seibel (2001). *The Nonprofit Sector in Germany. Between State, Economy and Society*. Manchester and New York: Manchester University Press.

Boeßenecker, Karl-Heinz and Michael Vilain (2013). *Spitzenverbände der Freien Wohlfahrtspflege*, Weinheim: Beltz/Juventus.

Bundesarbeitsgemeinschaft der Freien Wohlfahrtspflege (2018). *Gesamtstatistik, Berlin:7:* https://www.bagfw.de/fileadmin/user_upload/Veroeffentlichungen/Pub likationen/Statistik/BAGFW_Gesamtstatistik_2016.pdf.

Enquete-Kommission "Zukunft des Bürgerschaftlichen Engagements" Deutscher Bundestag (2002). *Bericht. Bürgerschaftliches Engagement: auf dem Weg in eine zukunftsfähige Bürgergesellschaft*, Opladen: Leske+Budrich.

Freise, Matthias und Annette Zimmer (2004). "Der Dritte Sektor im wohlfahrtsstaatlichen Arrangement." In Aurel Croissant et al. (eds.): *Wohlfahrtsstaatliche Politik in jungen Demokratien*, Wiesbaden: VS Verlag, 153–172.

Kausmann, Corinna et al. (2019). "Zivilgesellschaftliches Engagement." In Holger Krimmer (ed.): *Datenreport Zivilgesellschaft*, Wiesbaden: Springer VS, 55–91 (Open Access).

Krimmer, Holger (2019). "Summary. Zivilgesellschaft im Überblick." In Holger Krimmer (ed.): *Datenreport Zivilgesellschaft*, Wiesbaden: Springer VS, online available at: https://www.ziviz.de/datenreport-zivilgesellschaft.

Krimmer, Holger (eds.) (2021). *Datenreport Zivilgesellschaft*, Wiesbaden: Springer VS (forthcoming).

Priemer, Jana et al. (2019). "Organisierte Zivilgesellschaft." In Holger Krimmer (ed.): *Datenreport Zivilgesellschaft*, Wiesbaden: Springer VS: 7–45, online available at: https://www.ziviz.de/datenreport-zivilgesellschaft.

Priller, Eckhard et al. (2012). *Dritte-Sektor-Organisationen heute: Eigene Ansprüche und ökonomische Herausforderungen*. Berlin: WZB, online available at: https://www.ssoar.info/ssoar/handle/document/46175.

Salamon, Lester M. et al. (eds.) (1999). *Global Civil Society. Dimensions of the Nonprofit Sector*, Baltimore: Center for Civil Society Studies.

Simonson, Julia et al. (2017). "Zentrale Ergebnisse des Deutschen Freiwilligensurvey 2014." In Julia Simonson, Claudia Vogel, Clemens Tesch-Römer (eds.). *Freiwilliges Engagement in Deutschland*, Wiesbaden: Springer VS, online available at: https://www.bmfsfj.de/blob/113702/53d7fdc57ed97e4124fffec0ef5562a1/vierter-f reiwilligensurvey-monitor-data.pdf.

Zimmer, Annette et al. (2004). "The Legacy of Subsidiarity: The Nonprofit Sector in Germany" In Annette Zimmer and Eckhard Priller (eds.). *Future of Civil Society*, Wiesbaden: VS-Verlag, 681–711.

Zimmer, Annette and Eckhard Priller (2007). *Gemeinnützige Organisationen im gesellschaftlichen Wandel*. Wiesbaden: VS-Verlag.

Zimmer, Annette and Franziska Paul (2018). "Zur volkswirtschaftlichen Bedeutung der Sozialwirtschaft." In Klaus Grunwald and Andreas Langer (eds.). *Sozialwirtschaft*, Baden-Baden: Nomos, 103–118.

Zimmer, Annette and Eckhard Priller (2019). "Genossenschaften als Teil des Dritten Sektors", *Zeitschrift für öffentliche und gemeinwirtschaftliche Unternehmen*, 42:3, 280–299.

Zimmer, Annette and Eckhard Priller, Helmut K. Anheier, Helmut K. (2013). "Der Nonprofit Sektor in Deutschland." In Ruth Simsa, Michael Meyer and Christophf Badelt (eds.). *Handbuch der Nonprofit-Organisation*, Stuttgart: Poeschel Verlag, 15–36.

Models of Public Administration and German Subsidiarity

Annette Zimmer and Christina Grabbe

1 Introduction

Germany is the home country of Max Weber, the author of a seminal work on modern bureaucracy. It is a federal state in which municipalities have always played a key administrative role, particularly with respect to social service provision. Finally, it is a country traditionally characterised as a neo-corporatist (Schmitter 1974) or "semi-sovereign state" (Katzenstein 1987), in which private actors have always been thoroughly integrated into governance arrangements. Taken together, Germany has very distinct traditions of a) public administration, b) local self-government and c) public–private cooperation, conceptualised as "subsidiarity" in the domain of public social service provision (see Lovelady and Grabbe 2019).

With a focus on Germany, this article provides a concise overview of these different traditions and models of public administration. In recent decades, there have been profound changes to the modes of government and governance in the country. This has had a significant impact on the role and function of non-profit organisations that provide social services primarily at the local level of governance in Germany. This local-level government and non-profit cooperation was the key focus of the LoGoSO project. After presenting an overview of the different models of public administration, this article focuses explicitly on the local level by outlining the tradition of German self-government that significantly impacted the development of the German welfare state, in particular the development of the so-called "dual system" of social service provision. Against this background, the article will examine the nexus between local self-government and subsidiary social service provision. The traditional position of the German Welfare Associations, as the central providers of social services, will be highlighted and explained in reference to the fact that subsidiarity used to be a component of German social laws. The article concludes with a discussion of the current state of service provision in Germany. Non-profits are still key partners of German local governments. However, they enjoy a far less privileged role today than in the past. There has also been a significant increase in the variety and complexity of both the supply side of social service providers and the demand side of local governments and how they cooperate with the providers and regulate the provision of services.

2 From Bureaucracy to New Public Governance

2.1 The Bureaucracy Model

"Everything must change, if everything is to stay as it is." This famous quote from the novel Il Gattopardo might serve as a metaphor for the outcome of the different waves of reform and modernisation in German public administration. In Germany, public administration was almost exclusively a sub-discipline of legal scholarship. Accordingly, public administration at each level of government was the prime domain of professionals with a background in jurisprudence. The set-up, or internal structures, of public administration followed the blueprint that Max Weber characterised as "modern bureaucracy". This model of public administration stands out for the following features:

- "the dominance of the rule of law;
- a focus on administering set rules and guidelines;
- a central role for the bureaucracy in policy making and implementation;
- the 'politics-administration' split within public organisations;
- a commitment to incremental budgeting; and
- the hegemony of the professional in public service delivery" (Osborne 2013, 418).

From the late 19th century onwards, Germany was a prime example of a form of public administration that reflected the concept of a strong state/government with pronounced steering capacity. Hierarchy was perceived as the most efficient mode of coordination; and the departments of public administration were exclusively run by professionals, trained in jurisprudence and acted in accordance with departmental records and files. Also, for decades, the hierarchical bureaucratic model of public administration was regarded as the most efficient and effective public administration approach (Bogumil and Jann 2009).

2.2 The New Public Management Model

Against this background, it came as a shock that the results of international comparative research revealed significant deficiencies in German public administration. Studies comparing local public administration in different countries indicated that, particularly at the local level of government, Germany's traditional bureaucratic administrative approach no longer corresponded to the needs of modern times (Bertelsmann-Stiftung 1993, 1994). The reaction to this revelation was at least twofold. First, the academic community of public administration broadened its approach by opening up to concepts from economics, policy analysis and business administration. At the shop-floor level, public administrators all over the country, advised by policy experts and professional associations, embraced techniques and instruments of New Public Management (NPM). In a short time, NPM developed into the new model of public administration in Germany in the 1990s (Holtkamp 2010, chapter 9; Kleinfeld 1996; Reichard 1994). To replace "hierarchy" with "the market" as the central mode of coordination is the central idea of NPM, whose prime features were summarised by Christopher Hood as follows:

- "Hands-on professional management in the public sector;
- explicit standards and measures of performance;
- greater emphasis on output controls;
- shift to a disaggregation of units in the public sector;
- shift to greater competition in public sector;
- stress on private-sector styles of management practice;
- stress on greater discipline and parsimony in resource use." (Hood 1991, 4f).

Consequently, NPM introduced business administration instruments and management techniques to the public sector or, to put it differently, NPM led to the partial managerialisation of the public sector (Maier et al. 2016). The reason for the popularity of NPM is related to the fact that worldwide management techniques of business administration are increasingly perceived as being superior to those of traditional bureaucracy and therefore better suited to the improvement of the quality, efficiency and effectiveness of public administration (Osborne 2006, 378; Bogumil and Jann 2009, 239). However, it is worth underlining that NPM does not stand for a coherent theoretical or conceptual approach. Instead, it might be characterised as a toolbox of various instruments and techniques that can be utilised as appropriate (Drechsler and Radma-Liiv 2015, 33).

Accordingly, it is useful to distinguish between a) the application of NPM techniques within the core units of public administration, e.g. at the departmental level, and b) the use of NPM techniques for the management of external relations and/or public service production of the respective governmental unit. The latter led to a wave of privatisation and the crowding-out of activities and services that used to be organised publicly. By the mid-1980s, the privatisation of public industries—e.g. television, telephone, railroads, public utilities—began. While the UK took the lead, Germany wasn't far behind. This initial wave of privatisation was then followed by a second one in the 1990s that aimed at remodelling the welfare state. In a nutshell, public organisations operating in prime welfare domains, such as healthcare, education and care for children or the elderly, were transformed into private entities through a change of their legal form, while the government and/or social insurance providers continued to be responsible for financing those services.

As outlined elsewhere, the privatisation of formerly "core" public administration activities in the domains of welfare and education translated into the significant growth of the non-profit sector. This was due to the fact that in many countries, and particularly in the UK, either public social service providers were, through a change in their legal status, transformed into non-profit organisations or the government outsourced social service activities to existing non-profits (Kendall and Knapp 1996; Deakin 2001). However, in sharp contrast to other highly developed welfare states, this shift in social service provision from public to non-profit providers wasn't a key issue in Germany because the German welfare state never replaced private non-profit social service providers with state-run services (Zimmer 2019). Non-profit organisations were already heavily involved in the provision of social services, so there was no need for privatisation in favour of non-profits. Nevertheless, as will be outlined in the next sections, the introduction of NPM significantly changed the relationships and modes of co-operation between public administration authorities and non-profit organisations in Germany. However, with very few exceptions (Wollmann 2016; Henriksen et al. 2016), this has not been a key issue in public administration research and discourse.

Instead, German academic discourse has focused on the transformation of the internal structures of public administration triggered by NPM. Particularly, NPM inspired the reform of local public administration bodies (Holtkamp 2012; Reichard 1994; Reichard and Wollmann 1996). However, it soon became clear that NPM aspirations may have been too far-reaching, and therefore implementation proved to be too time-consuming and costly. Also, critical voices pointed out that the reforms under the leitmotif of NPM were too inward bound and that they neglected to consider the needs and demands of the citizens. To make a long story short, the units of public administration were not completely transformed into organisations that mimic commercial enterprises. Instead, with the rise of the new leitmotif of public administration—"governance"—the external relations of local public administration departments became the centre of attention, in particular their relationship with citizens who utilise public services (Bogumil et al. 2003; Oppen et al. 2005; Holtkamp 2005). Accordingly, reforms with a focus on the internal procedures of public administration were downsized in Germany. More and more, reform aspirations were guided by the idea that access to core public services, such as residence registration or passport application, should be easier for local citizens. Simultaneously, there was re-acceptance of bureaucracy as a mode of steering public administration and, as such, internal administration continued to be managed hierarchically, guided by the rule of law and organised in accordance with departmental records and files. Today, there is no doubt that the bureaucracy model is still firmly in place. The traditional bureaucratic steering mechanisms continue to be key characteristics of public administration in this country, which may, however, be partially modified by or supplemented with NPM instruments.

2.3 The New Public Governance Model

Currently, "new public governance" constitutes the third and most recent paradigm, or model, of public administration to come after the models of "bureaucracy" and "New Public Management". In contrast to NPM, new public governance is less inward-focused and not centred on the internal re-structuring of administration. Instead, as a new leitmotif, it is a shift towards a form of public administration that is more engaged in partnerships, networks and contractual relations with a variety of partners (Dossi 2017, 33) including public, non-profit and commercial entities (Polzer 2016, 47). These relationships and networks might be restricted to the production and provision of services; however, private actors might also participate in policy development processes including agenda setting at the local, regional and national levels of government (Haus and Kuhlmann 2013, see chapter 3).

The public administration research community perceives "governance" predominantly as a normative concept, referenced under various labels such as "citizen-centered governance, [...] networked governance" (Hartley 2005) or "public governance" (Pollitt and Bouckaert 2017), which highlights the participatory or network component of current public administration. For the purposes of this article, Osborne's (2006) designation of "new public governance" is preferred and encompasses both a policy-implementation and a policymaking component. Accordingly, he characterises "new public governance" as a mode of governing that covers two distinct meanings: "a plural state, where multiple interdependent actors (that) contribute to the delivery of public services and a pluralist state, where multiple processes inform the public policy making system" (Osborne 2006, 384)

Due to the German tradition of local self-government, which served as an incubator for the development of "subsidiarity" as a special form of public–private partnership in this country, basically a variant of "new public governance", the third paradigm of public administration is indeed not so new to the German context. This will be outlined in more detail in the next chapters with an overview of both the tradition of local self-government and "subsidiarity" that constitutes the normative underpinning of the traditional mode of close cooperation between local public administration authorities and non-profit organisations in the area of social service provision.

3 Local Self-Government and Subsidiarity

3.1 Tradition and Reality of Local Self-Government

Germany looks back upon a long tradition of local self-government. In contrast to the UK and France, where public policy design and administration was centralised and located in the capital, the Prussian government took a different developmental path at the beginning of the 19th century. Due to severe fiscal problems in the aftermath of the Napoleonic Wars, the Prussian government tried to limit its spending by delegating the bulk of public tasks to the local level and hence to municipalities. Ever since, at least from a legal point of view, German municipalities have been entities that both governed and were responsible for themselves. In theory, German communities are supposed to be able to finance their programmes and policies independently since they are allowed to collect land, income and business taxes.

Depending on the overall economic situation of the region and the respective community, German local governments are more or less in good financial shape. Furthermore, in contrast to the early years of local self-administration, today's German municipalities constitute, first and foremost, the lowest level of public administration in the country; they are primarily responsible for the implementation of policies and laws designed at the national and German *Länder* (state/regional) levels of government. In international comparisons, current German public administration is characterised as a 'continental European fused system' (Kuhlmann and Wollmann 2014, 98), in which the different levels (European, national, regional and local) work closely together. It is a system labelled "cooperative federalism" by the German political scientist Fritz Scharpf (1976), meaning that each level of government is closely bound together and forced to cooperate.

Although, German municipalities operate in a highly regulated administrative system, they still enjoy some leeway to design programmes or interpret policy measures as they please. This is particularly true for policy areas earmarked as "voluntary tasks" and regulated under the legislative authority of the *Länder*. The policy areas of arts and culture, leisure and education fall into this category. However, for the majority of welfare-related policy areas, such as health or social services (e.g. care for the elderly or children), municipalities have to comply with national policy. Nevertheless, they still have flexibility in regard to the degree of their financial engagement and their options when implementing that policy. Depending on the financial situation of each respective municipality, national policy programmes might be put in place with generous funding or, in contrast, only funded with the bare minimum allowed by law. Scholars of public administration therefore indicate that self-government of Germany's municipalities corresponds to the 'local administration-centred integration model' (Wollmann 1999, 196), since they still enjoy the right to regulate all matters for the local community under their responsibility (Kuhlmann and Wollmann 2014, 75), although they are thoroughly integrated into a rigidly regulated system in which they primarily serve as policy implementers.

3.2 The Dual System of Local Social Service Provision

There is a close nexus between the German tradition of local self-government and the country's current "welfare mix" (Evers 1995), in which non-profit organisations play a very prominent role (Bode 2004; Zimmer 2019, 41ff). Germany's welfare state and, in particular, the provision of public social services were not exclusively designed "from above". Instead the typical German arrangement, the so-called "dual system" of private non-profit and public social service provision, came into being at the local level and, hence, was an outcome of self-government.

Early in the 19th century, the Prussian government very successfully integrated and utilised the new social classes of wealthy citizens, entrepreneurs, industrialists and merchants. Under the framework of local self-government, those well-to-do male members of the community, who served as elected members of city councils, became responsible for governing municipal affairs. In other words, they had to run the city and also make sure that the community was in good financial shape. Against this background, beyond their service as members of the city council, many of their positions in local public administration were honorary. And even when local administrations became increasingly professionalised, alongside industrialisation and the growth of cities, quite a few tasks, particularly in the welfare domain, continued to be practices without any financial compensation.

The city of Wuppertal in the north-west of Germany is a textbook example. Based on its textile industry, the city was one of the richest municipalities in the former German Empire. Wuppertal was also the hometown of Friedrich Engels, the most important supporter of Karl Marx. In Wuppertal, welfare, or more specifically pauper relief, was decentralised and organised locally in community quarters, where volunteers took care of a limited number of very poor people and their families (Hammerschmidt 2011, 25). The volunteers were members of the middle classes and it was their responsibility to help poor families to get by and find a job. This so-called "Elberfelder System", privately organised social service provision, developed into a widely used and frequently copied model in German cities at that time. In the second half of the 19th century, like in other highly industrialised countries, members of the middle classes founded local initiatives with the aim of helping the poor and needy in fast-growing industrial centres. These non-profit welfare organisations, e.g. hospitals, orphanages or homes for vulnerable groups, were privately financed social enterprises, predominantly run by volunteers (Sachße 2011; Zimmer and Obuch 2017).

Simultaneously, in the booming industrial regions of Germany, municipalities began to establish facilities and programmes with the dual goal of helping the poor and integrating newcomers, who were by and large migrant workers flooding into the metropolitan areas. Since the general authority (Allzuständigkeit) of the municipalities was the legal rule, German municipalities were required by law to take care of everything within their regional domain. Against this background, problems and difficulties related to accelerated industrialisation and urbanisation, such as deficits in terms of the provision of local infrastructure, social services and welfare, or the so-called "social question", propelled the growth and professionalisation of local administration and public utilities in Germany (Hammerschmidt 2011, 27).

However, in contrast to other industrialised countries, the developing German welfare state did not absorb the "private culture of welfare". It did not take service provision out of the hands of the numerous, mostly local, volunteer-run non-profit organisations that were heavily engaged in social service and healthcare provision (Sachße 1996). Instead, from a very early stage onwards, "public welfare" coordinated its activities with "private welfare" resulting in a 'dual system' (Sachße 1995) of social service provision, a system where public organisations worked almost on par, and in close cooperation, with "private welfare", i.e. local non-profit organisations and their umbrellas, the famous German Welfare Associations (Boeßenecker and Vilain 2013, see footnote2).

3.3 Subsidiarity as a Variant of Neo-Corporatism

According to Philippe Schmitter's classical definition, "neo-corporatism" refers to a policy or "ideal-typical institutional arrangement" where societal organisations have a prominent voice in policy planning processes or within the "decisional structures of the state" (Schmitter 1974, 86). A second important feature of neo-corporatism highlighted by Schmitter relates to the limited number of actors involved in neo-corporatist arrangements. Furthermore, these actors have to be "recognized and licensed (if not created) by the state" (Schmitter 1974, 94). As such, neo-corporatism stands in direct contrast to pluralist arrangements, which are based on a plurality of actors in which the state does not significantly interfere.

For decades, political scientists categorised Germany as a neo-corporatist country. The history of neo-corporatism dates back to the times of the German Empire (Kleinfeld 2007). By and large, research on neo-corporatism focused on the economy and therefore on the cooperation between the associations of "capital" and "labour", trade unions and employers and/or business associations. However, starting in the 1980s, policy research identified further arenas where the mode of cooperative government had significant neo-corporatist features, characterised by a restricted number of private actors working closely with the government and public administration in both processes of policy planning and policy implementation (Katzenstein 1987).

In a widely cited article, the German sociologists Rolf G. Heinze and Thomas Olk (1981) convincingly argued that the welfare domain, specifically public social service provision, is a policy area that displays strong features of neo-corporatism. In particular, a limited number of associations, representing specific constituencies of German society, are recognised and licenced by the government as umbrellas to cooperate with public institutions at every level of Germany's federal system in both policy planning and policy implementation. These societal organisations, which enjoy such a privileged position in Germany's welfare state, are the Welfare Associations (Boeßenecker and Vilain 2013). Again, their history dates back to the time of the German Empire; they were and still are the most important providers of social services in Germany. Their remarkable success at maintaining their position as partners of the government in policy planning and implementation, as well as key providers of social services, is closely linked to both their embeddedness in German society and the very specific interpretation of the principle of subsidiarity that prioritised the incorporation of these organisations into the developing German welfare state (Schmid 1996; Zimmer 2019).

According to the welfare state typology of Esping-Andersen (1990), there are two features of social service provision in Germany that formerly set the country apart from both the liberal, pluralistic and the social democratic, centralised model of the welfare state: 1) the exclusive 'dual system' of public non-profit social service provision that, for a long time, excluded any commercial providers; and 2) the neo-corporatist approach to social policy planning and implementation that was legitimised by the incorporation of the principle of subsidiarity (Sachße 2003) into German social laws and gave the Welfare Associations a privileged position as partners in policymaking and policy implementation.

As early as the beginning of the last century, and alongside the growth of the German welfare state, the 'dual system' of public and private non-profit welfare (Sachße 1995) operating primarily at the local level of municipalities, was 'uploaded' to the national level of government. It was firmly established by the support of the developing German welfare bureaucracy and the umbrella associations of the local non-profit social service providers, the Welfare Associations (Sachße 1995). From an economic point of view, the Welfare Associations are still the most important providers of social services in Germany (Zimmer/Paul 2018). They grew out of Germany's traditional social milieus, which structured German society up until the 1970s (Hammerschmidt 2005).

When societal modernisation started in the late 19th century, Germany's society was very heterogeneous. There were strong societal cleavages, organised along specific social milieus of which the 'Catholic', the 'Protestant' and the 'social democratic' milieus were the most prominent. Non-profit organisations constituted the organisational infrastructure of these milieus, which were vertically integrated by 'umbrella associations' organised along the aforementioned normative and religious cleavages and bound together by norms and values. This pattern of societal structuration, also characterised as "pillarisation", was not restricted to the social domain; it was also very prevalent in sports or other leisure-oriented areas (Zimmer 1999). From the very beginning, the 'umbrellas' and the local non-profits agreed upon a division of labour: 'Umbrellas' operating at the national and regional levels of government were primarily active in policy planning, lobbying activities and bargaining procedures; their membership organisations at the local level were primarily responsible for service provision, most of which was accomplished by volunteers, at least in the early years of the welfare state.

In the welfare domain, the extraordinary success story of the Welfare Associations was closely linked to the interpretation of the 'principle of subsidiarity' in Germany. Based on Catholic social doctrine, the principle was originally designed to protect individual rights against any powerful intervention from the state. After World War II, the principle was incorporated into German social laws and redefined in favour of the Welfare Associations. Local governments were, by law, not allowed to establish a public social service facility as long as a non-profit organisation affiliated with the Welfare Associations was able to provide the service. The subsidiarity-based primacy of non-profit service provision also prohibited commercial competition in the welfare domain. As a result, up until major policy changes in the 1990s, non-profits providing social services were protected from for-profit competition, worked closely with public organisations in the areas of social service and healthcare provision, and, like their public counterparts, were protected from bankruptcy.

4 Social Service Provision Today

Since the 1990s, the distinct features of the German welfare state, particularly the dual system of social service production, have changed significantly. First, the national government established cost containment strategies for every area of social service provision. As part of this overall effort, the deficits of social service and healthcare providers are no longer offset with public subsidies at the end of the fiscal year. Second, the national government modified the "principle of subsidiarity" by allowing organisations not affiliated with the traditional Welfare Associations to operate in the welfare domain, including independent non-profits and, more important-ly, commercial providers. Just like the membership organisations of the Welfare Associations, these new actors became eligible to obtain public grants and contracts (Backhaus-Maul and Olk 1994). Third, municipalities, faced with severe fiscal constraints, increasingly outsourced cost-intensive care facilities, which was particularly true for community hospitals that were sold to private companies (Zimmer 2009).

As a result of these measures, the welfare mix of social service provision has changed significantly and private for-profit providers gained an in-creasing share of the healthcare and social services markets in Germany (Zimmer and Smith 2014). Accordingly, the "dual system", which was re-stricted to public and non-profit service providers, developed into a plural-istic system of various actors, including commercial firms, the Welfare As-sociations and their membership organisations operating locally, a small number of social enterprises, and non-profits which are not affiliated with the Welfare Associations.

With respect to financing, the legal form of the service provider does not matter. Reimbursements (Leistungsentgelte) for service provision con-stitute the most important revenue source for social service and healthcare organisations in Germany. The government does not regulate the amount of money allocated for a single service. Instead, the amount of money pro-vided as reimbursement per capita, or per service, is the result of a bargain-ing process between representatives of regulating, financing and service provision entities. The participants in these bargaining processes are repre-sentatives of insurance funds, municipalities and service providers—non-profit and for-profit. This translates into a situation in which "prizes" for social services vary depending on the financial prosperity of those covering the costs of the service (municipalities, social and health insurance providers).

Besides reimbursements, social service providers are eligible to receive government grants. Traditionally, these were allocated either as annual payments or on demand. However, eligibility was previously restricted to non-profit organisations affiliated with the Welfare Associations. Today, every legally acknowledged social service provider is eligible to apply for government grants or to receive subsidies. Not only is there a much larger pool of organisations eligible to seek grants or public subsidies now that it isn't restricted to the Welfare Associations, but there has also been a change in how public monies are granted and monitored. In accordance with the rise of New Public Management in the 1990s, local governments introduced competitive tendering and contract management to distribute and monitor public funds.

However, NPM did not thoroughly replace former modes of governance in the welfare domain. Compared to previous times, there is a far greater plurality of providers—public, non-profit, commercial—that receive funds and grants for the supply of social services. But in contrast to the leitmotif of NPM, local public administration authorities do not exclusively rely on mechanisms of competition, such as competitive tendering, in Germany. Instead, modes of governance differ depending on the policy area, the local tradition, the availability of funds for a local community or the overall culture of the particular local government and public administration body. Without doubt, the legacy of a long tradition of cooperation with the membership organisations of the Welfare Associations continues to have an impact. Furthermore, German public administration is still highly departmentalised and organised in accordance with Max Weber's bureaucratic model. This is certainly a challenge in times of stress and work overload, when new problems or new clients and/or constituencies, such as refugees and migrants, ask for intensified attention and support. Indeed, empirical research and analysis are needed to understand how German public administration operates in the area of public service provision. More research is needed to determine if instruments of new public management are strongly in place or less favoured and whether, and to what extent, private actors, in particular non-profit organisations, are welcome to participate in processes of policy creation. Or in contrast, it might also be the case that non-profit organisations are solely perceived as providers of services that enlarge their field of operation by applying for government grants or by taking part in processes of bidding for contracts, issued and monitored by the local administration authority.

5 Summary

The purpose of this article was to provide an overview of the reform models of public administration in Germany and to analyse, with a special focus on non-profit organisations, their impact on the provision of social services. It was outlined that New Public Management, as a prominent reform model of public administration, did not replace the traditional bureaucracy model. Germany's public authorities are still strongly departmentalised hierarchical organisations. However, instruments of NPM are widely utilised by German public authorities in the management of external relations. In the NPM model, government programmes and grants are provided on a competitive basis and they are monitored and evaluated using techniques of business administration. However, the shift towards the most recent model of public administration—new public governance—is not the primary reason why the majority of social services in Germany, particularly at the local level in municipalities, are provided by private organisations and not public ones.

As outlined, Germany's social policy activities that regulate local government and private non-profit engagement in communities on behalf of the needy and the poor are the main factors that created the current social service provision structure. However, for decades local governments only cooperated with a very limited number of social service providers, the membership organisations of the Welfare Associations. As indicated, this exclusive partnership was backed by two distinct German traditions, namely local self-government translating into a general responsibility among municipalities for all matters in their domain, and the so-called semi-sovereignty of the German state, which constitutes a synonym for neo-corporatist policy formation and implementation. While local self-government, albeit modified and embedded into a highly regulated system of "cooperative federalism", is still in place in Germany, neo-corporatism, particularly its special variant of subsidiarity, no longer dominates the mode of governance in the domain of public social service provision. Today, there is a multitude of service providers with very different legal forms that are eligible to partner local governments. This new situation has a significant impact on non-profit organisations. Non-profits face increased competition from for-profit providers. Moreover, there are multiple modes of how local governments and their public administration bodies cooperate with private—commercial or non-profit—providers of social services. The Lo-GoSO project addressed the topic of how local governments cooperated with non-profit organisations in selected cities and policy areas with the aim of integrating newcomers, refugees and asylum seekers into the local community with the help of social services (see Lovelady and Grabbe 2019).

References

Backhaus-Maul, Holger and Thomas Olk (1994). "Von Subsidiarität zu „outcontracting": Zum Wandel der Beziehungen zwischen Staat und Wohlfahrtsverbänden in der Sozialpolitik" In Wolfgang Streeck (ed.) *Staat und Verbände*, Wiesbaden: Westdeutscher Verlag, 100-135.

Bertelsmann-Stiftung (1993). *Demokratie und Effizienz in der Kommunalverwaltung. Band I. Dokumentenband zur internationalen Recherche.* Gütersloh: Bertelsmann Verlag.

Bertelsmann-Stiftung (1994). *Demokratie und Effizienz in der Kommunalverwaltung. Band II. Dokumentation zu Symposium und Festakt.* Gütersloh: Bertelsmann Verlag.

Bode, Ingo (2014). *Disorganisierter Wohlfahrtskapitalismus Die Reorganisation des Sozialsektors in Deutschland, Frankreich und Großbritannien.* Wiesbaden: Springer VS.

Boeßenecker, Karl-Heinz and Michael Vilain (2013). *Spitzenverbände der Freien Wohlfahrtspflege.* Weinheim: Beltz-Verlag.

Bogumil, Jörg and Jann, Werner (2009). *Verwaltung und Verwaltungswissenschaft in Deutschland. Einführung in die Verwaltungswissenschaft*, 2nd Edition. Wiesbaden: VS Verlag für Sozialwissenschaften.

Bogumil, Jörg and Lars Holtkamp, Gudrun Schwarz (eds.) (2003). *Das Reformmodell Bürgerkommune.* Berlin: edition sigma.

Deakin, Nicholas (2001). "Putting narrow-mindedness out of countenance: the UK voluntary sector in the new millennium". In: Helmut K. Anheier and Jeremy Kendall (eds.) *The Third Sector Policy at the Crossroads*, London/New York: Routledge, 36-50.

Dossi, Samuele (2017). *Cities and the European Union. Mechanisms and modes of Europeanisation*, Colchester: European Consortium for Political Research.

Drechsler, Wolfgang and Tiina Randma-Liiv (2015). "The New Public Management Then and Now: Lessons from the Transition in Central and Eastern Europe". In: Michiel S. De Vries and Juraj Nemec (eds.) *Implementation of New Public Management Tools. Experiences from Transition and Emerging Countries*, Brussels: Bruyland, 33-49.

Evers, Adalbert (1995). "Part of the Welfare Mix: The Third Sector as an Intermediate Arena", *Voluntas* 6:2, 159–182.

Hammerschmidt, Peter (2005). *Wohlfahrtsverbände in der Nachkriegszeit. Reorganisation und Finanzierung der Spitzenverbände der freien Wohlfahrtspflege 1945 bis 1961*, Weinheim/München: Juventa.

Hammerschmidt, Peter (2011). „Kommunale Selbstverwaltung und kommunale Sozialpolitik – ein historischer Überblick". In: Heinz-Jürgen Dahme and Norbert Wohlfahrt (eds.) *Handbuch Kommunale Sozialpolitik*, Wiesbaden: VS Verlag, 21-40.

Hartley, Jean (2005). "Innovation in Governance and Public Services: Past and Present", *Public Money and Management*, 25:1, 27–34.

Haus, Michael and Sabine Kuhlmann (eds.) (2013). *Lokale Politik im Zeichen der Krise?* Wiesbaden: Springer VS.

Heinze, Rolf G. and Thomas Olk (1981). "Die Wohlfahrtsverbände im System sozialer Dienstleistungsproduktion", *Kölner Zeitschrift für Soziologie und Sozialsychologie*, 33, 94–114.

Henriksen, Lars Skov and Steven Rathgeb Smith, Malene Thøgersen, Annette Zimmer (2016). "On the Road to Marketization? A Comparative Analysis of Nonprofit Sector Involvement in Social Service Delivery at the Local Level". In: Sabine Kuhlmann and Geert Bouckaert (eds.) *Local Public Sector Reforms in Times of Crises*, edited by, London: Palgrave/Macmillan, 221-236.

Holtkamp, Lars (2005). "Lokale Governance". In: Arthur Benz, Susanne Lütz, Uwe Schimank, Georg Simonis (ed.) *Handbuch Governance*, Wiesbaden: VS Verlag, 366-377.

Holtkamp, Lars (2012). *Verwaltungsreformen. Problemorientierte Einführung in die Verwaltungswissenschaft.* Wiesbaden: Springer VS.

Hood, Christopher (1991). "A Public Management for all Seasons", *Public Administration*", 69:1, 3–19.

Katzenstein, Peter J. (1987). *Policy and Politics in West-Germany: The Growth of a Semisovereign State.* Philadelphia: Temple University Press.

Kendall, Jeremy and Knapp, Martin (1996). *The voluntary sector in the UK.* Manchester: Manchester University Press.

Kleinfeld, Ralf (2007). „Die historische Entwicklung der Interessenverbände in Deutschland". In: Thomas von Winter and Ulrich Willems (eds.) *Interessenverbände in Deutschland*, Wiesbaden: VS-Verlag, 51-83.

Kleinfeld, Ralf (1996). *Kommunalpolitik.* Opladen: Leske+Budrich.

Kuhlmann, Sabine and Hellmuth Wollmann (2014). *Introduction to Comparative Public Administration. Administrative Systems and Reforms in Europe.* Cheltenham: Edgar Elgar.

Lovelady, Beth and Christina Grabbe (2019). "Models of Co-operation in Germany's Migrant Services", *LoGoSo Working Paper*, online available at: http://dx.doi.org/10.17169/refubium-26559.

Maier, Florentine and Michael Meyer, Martin Steinbereithner (2016). Nonprofit Organizations Becoming Business-Like: A Systematic Review. *Nonprofit and Voluntary Sector Quarterly*, 45:1, 64–86.

Oppen, Maria and Detlef Sack, Alexander Wegener (eds.) (2005). *Abschied von der Binnenmodernisierung? Kommunen zwischen Wettbewerb und Kooperation.* Berlin: edition sigma.

Osborne, Stephen P. (2006). "The New Public Governance?", *Public Management Review*, 8:3, 377–387.

Osborne, Stephen. P. (2013). "Public Governance and Public Services: A Brave New World or New Wine in Old Bottles?" In: Tom Christensen and Per Lægreid (eds.) *The Ashgate Research Companion to New Public Management*, Burlington, England: Ashgate, 417-430.

Pollitt, Christopher and Geert Bouckaert (2017). *Public Management Reform: A Comparative Analysis – Into the Age of Austerity*, 4. Edition, Oxford: Oxford University.

Polzer, Tobias (2016). *Von klassischer Verwaltung zu Public Governance. Rolle von Verwaltungsparadigmen in Reformen des öffentlichen Rechnungswesens*. Wiesbaden: Springer VS.

Reichard, Christoph (1994). *Umdenken im Rathaus: Neue Steuerungsmodelle in der deutschen Kommunalverwaltung*, Berlin: edition sigma.

Reichard, Christoph and Hellmuth Wollmann (eds.) (1996). *Kommunalverwaltungen im Modernisierungsschub?*. Basel: Birkhäuser Verlag.

Sachße, Christoph (1995). "Verein, Verband und Wohlfahrtsstaat. Entstehung und Entwicklung der dualen Wohlfahrtspflege". In: Thomas Rauschenbach, Christoph Sachße, Christoph and Thomas Olk (eds.) *Von der Wertegemeinschaft zum Dienstleistungsunternehmen*, Frankfurt: Suhrkamp, 123-149.

Sachße, Christoph (1996). "Public and Private in German Social Welfare". In: Michael B. Katz and Christoph Sachße (eds.) *The Mixed Economy of Welfare. Public/private relations in England, Germany and the United States, the 1870's to the 1930's*, Baden-Baden: Nomos, 148-169.

Sachße, Christoph (2003). "Subsidiarität: Leitmaxime deutscher Wohlfahrtsstaatlichkeit". In: Stephan Lessenich (ed.) *Wohlfahrtsstaatliche Grundbegriffe. Historische und aktuelle Diskurse*, Frankfurt am Main: Campus, 191–212.

Sachße, Christoph (2011). "Zur Geschichte sozialer Dienste in Deutschland". In: Adalbert Evers, Rolf G. Heinze, Thomas Olk (eds.) *Handbuch soziale Dienste*, Wiesbaden: VS Verlag, 94-116.

Scharpf, Fritz W. (1976). *Politikverflechtung. Theorie und Empirie des kooperativen Föderalismus in der Bundesrepublik*. Kronberg/Ts.: Scriptor Verlag.

Schmid, Josef (1996). *Wohlfahrtsverbände in modernen Wohlfahrtsstaaten. Soziale Dienste in historisch-vergleichender Perspektive*. Opladen: Leske+Budrich.

Schmitter, Philippe (1974). "Still the Century of Corporatism?" *The Review of Politics*, XXVI, 85–131.

Szeili, Judith and Annette Zimmer (2017). „Local Public Administration and Governance in Comparative Perspective", Berlin. LoGoSo Working Paper: https://logoso-project.com/publications/.

Wollmann, Hellmut (1999). 'Kommunalverwaltungen. Verwaltungsorgan oder Parlament?' In: Hellmut Wollmann, H. and Roland Roth (eds.) *Kommunalpolitik. Politisches Handeln in den Gemeinden*, Opladen: Leske + Budrich, 50-72.

Wollmann, Hellmut (2016). "Provision of Public and Social Services in European Countries: From Public Sector to Marketization and Reverse – or, What Next?" In: Sabine Kuhlmann and Geert Bouckaert (eds.) *Local Public Sector Reforms in Times of Crises*, London: Palgrave Macmillan, 187-204.

Zimmer, Annette (1999). "Corporatism Revisited – The Legacy of History and the German Nonprofit-Sector", *Voluntas*, 10:1, 37–49.

Zimmer, Annette (2009). "PPP im Krankenhausbereich: Das Universitätsklinikum Gießen – Marburg als Solitär", *Zeitschrift für Sozialreform*, 55:3, 253–273.

Zimmer, Annette (2019). "Wohlfahrtsstaatlichkeit in Deutschland: Tradition und Wandel der Zusammenarbeit mit zivilgesellschaftlichen Organisationen". In: Matthias Freise and Annette Zimmer (eds.) *Zivilgesellschaft und Wohlfahrtsstaat*, Wiesbaden: Springer VS, 32-54.

Zimmer, Annette and Katharina Obuch (2017). "A Matter of context? Understanding Social Enterprises in Changing Environments: The Case of Germany", *Voluntas*, 28:6: 2339–2359.

Zimmer, Annette and Franziska Paul (2018). "Zur volkswirtschaftlichen Bedeutung der Sozialwirtschaft". In: Klaus Grunwald and Andreas Langer (eds.) *Sozialwirtschaft*, Baden-Baden: Nomos, 103-118.

Zimmer, Annette and Steven Rathgeb Smith (2014). "Social Service Provision in the US and Germany: Convergence or Path Dependency?" *German Politics*, 23:1–2, 1–25.

Models of Cooperation in Germany's Migrant Services

Beth Lovelady and Christina Grabbe

1 Introduction

This paper investigates models of cooperation between the government and non-profit organisations (NPOs) in the policy area of migration in Germany as part of the LoGoSO project[1]. The cooperative relationships between local government and non-profits in Berlin and Cologne are evaluated from a new public governance perspective and considering the theories of third-party government and network governance. The specific instances of cooperation are compared using Coston's (1998) model of government-NPO relationships, which considers both formal and informal forms of cooperation. For the nine German case studies, we provide a summary of the relationship models found in migrant service provision in the cities of Berlin and Cologne. We then present two case studies that represent the most formal examples of third-party government and network governance.

2 Theoretical Framework of Government-NPO Cooperation

2.1 Cooperation and Public Administration

Research shows that cooperation between the state and the non-profit sector is not a recent phenomenon (Bode & Brandsen, 2014; Howlett, Kekez & Poocharoen, 2017). This is especially true in Germany, where local government began cooperating with NPOs at the end of the 19th century, in order to address challenges caused by urbanisation and industrialisation (Szeili & Zimmer, 2017; Zimmer & Grabbe 2020). The principle of sub-

---

1 Models of Cooperation between Local Governments and Social Organizations in Germany and China—Migration: Challenges and Solutions (LoGoSO Germany China) is a comparative research project conducted by the Freie Universität Berlin, the Westfälische Wilhelms Universität Münster and the Chinese Academy of Governance, funded by Stiftung Mercator. The duration of the research project was September 2016–August 2019.

sidiarity, along with the German constitutional designation of municipalities as the lowest administrative unit in the federal system, responsible for all community social issues, led to increased cooperation between local government and non-profits in the wake of the Second World War (Szeili & Zimmer, 2017). For decades, local government has looked to the German Welfare Associations as the main providers of services, and currently Welfare Associations represent over 100,000 entities that employ 1.7 million workers and 2.5 million volunteers (Szeili & Zimmer, 2017; Zimmer & Grabbe 2020).

It is no surprise, then, based upon this history of cooperation, that non-profit organisations play a key role in providing migrant services in Germany. Migration policy is a new field for local government and has very little regulation. Further, the recent arrival of large numbers of refugees has underscored the fact that municipalities are highly dependent on NPOs to deliver critical services (Szeili & Zimmer, 2017). While we are aware of this significant cooperation, there is little known about the nature of these cooperative relationships. Further, these relationships and the tools government utilises to engage with NPOs have likely been influenced by changes in prevailing public administration practices over the past several decades.

Public administration research lacks its own analytical concepts and, thus, employs those of other disciplines like systems theory or neo-institutionalism (Schnapp, 2006). One of these concepts, which is utilised in this paper is the creation of administrative paradigms. The paradigms can be seen as ideas and models of administrative reform that have been repeatedly voiced in a certain time period (Polzer, 2016). They describe "the organizing principles to guide reforms and practices, focus attention, give meaning to activities and specify what goals or values are to be pursued" (Meyer & Hammerschmid, 2006). Hartley (Hartley, 2005) identified three paradigms through which the public sector has passed since the post-World War II period. These are the bureaucracy—or simply (traditional) public administration (PA), new public management (NPM) and new public governance (NPG).

In the last few decades, governance practices have shifted from PA, a traditional concept of public administration that reflects a strong government which steers primarily through laws and regulations, towards NPM, which assumes that private-sector management techniques are superior to those of PA and focuses on improving the quality, efficiency and effectivity of public services (Bogumil, Jann & Nullmeier, 2006; Osborn, 2006; Polzer, 2016). The increased importance of NPM in the early 1990s, marketised service provision in Germany and, consequently, social laws were changed with the result that non-profit providers lost privileges in the system, allowing for-profit providers into the mix (Bode & Brandsen, 2014; Szeili & Zimmer, 2017; Zimmer & Grabbe 2020). However, while these changes created challenges for the social sector, non-profits remain an integral part of the German welfare system and its service provision.

The more recent paradigm shift towards NPG is the focus of this article (Howlett et al., 2017; Zimmer & Grabbe 2020). Contrary to PA and NPM, NPG is not centred on internal administrative processes and structures. Instead, it focuses on partnerships, networks and contracts between public administration and other actors (Dossi, 2017). These can span a variety of public, non-profit and commercial partners (Polzer, 2016).

In public administration research, "governance" is discussed not only as a research perspective but more as a normative concept categorised under various labels such as "citizen-centered governance, [...] networked governance" (Hartley, 2005) or "public governance" (Pollitt & Bouckaert, 2017). NPG, coined by Osborne in 2006, is a concept of governance where public, non-profit and commercial partners are involved in both policy implementation and policymaking.

For the government, non-public partners are a welcome addition to public management. Non-public partners help address ever-more complex social issues amidst increasingly constrained revenues (Bode & Brandsen, 2014; Pestoff, 2012). Under the NPG paradigm, NPOs are seen as key partners who bring the comparative advantages of additional resources (volunteers, donations) and close connections to specific user groups (Bode & Brandsen, 2014; Salamon, 1995). The resulting interaction between public administration and external actors under the NPG paradigm leads to various forms of governance, two of which are central to this study: third-party government and network governance.

2.2 Third-Party Government and Network Governance

Salamon defines third-party government as a system "in which government shares a substantial degree of its discretion over the spending of public funds and the exercise of public authority with third-party implementers" (1987, 37). This concept is strongly supportive of German subsidiarity in that it fulfils the government's obligation to set priorities on how to spend social resources while, at the same time, ensuring services are provided by those organisations closest to the problems being addressed. As previously mentioned, NPOs are well suited to this form of cooperation.

Two parts of Salamon's (1995) theory are key to understanding the occurrence of government–NPO cooperation. The first is the concept of 'voluntary failure', where NPOs provide services in response to market failures but lack the resources necessary to sufficiently respond to community needs. The second is that the government can solve problems more efficiently by cooperating with those already engaged in the work. Since NPOs are often first to respond to community needs (due to market failure), they already have programmes and structures in place so that once the community's needs exceed available NPO resources (voluntary failure) and rise to the level of government attention, cooperating with these NPOs provides a cost-effective mechanism for government response (Salamon, 1995).

The second model under the NPG paradigm which is closely tied to cooperative relationships in Germany is network governance. There is no commonly accepted theory with which to study the formation and function of networks (Torfing, 2014), but Torfing defines network governance as "networks of independent actors that contribute to the production of public governance" (2014, 99). Jones et al. are more exacting and define network governance as a specific group of autonomous 'firms' (including NPOs) that work together in order to successfully produce complex, highly customised services amid environmental uncertainty. Jones et al. also posit that network governance offers "comparative advantages over markets and hierarchies" (1997, 923), which aligns well with the NPG paradigm.

Networks can be either initiated by network partners themselves or—as is often the case in the public sector—can be mandated or contracted (Provan & Kenis, 2007). The preferred form of network interaction is frequent exchanges of knowledge, ideas and information that foster stronger ties between network partners (Jones, Hesterly & Borgatti, 1997; Torfing, 2014). Network partners maintain their autonomy, and, contrary to hierarchical modes of governance, participation in the network is voluntary. Although the network organisations might have different resources and structural positions that create asymmetric power relations, these power relations are horizontal, meaning that no actor can single-handedly resolve conflicts that emerge in the network.

Provan and Kenis (2007) further categorise networks along two dimensions. On the one hand, networks can be completely governed by the organisations that comprise the network. This results in a situation in which all organisations densely interact with each other and share governance. At the other extreme, the network can be managed by a single organisation. This leaves few direct organisation-to-organisation interactions, except for the purposes of operational issues such as the transfer of clients or information on services.

2.3 Coston's Model of Government–NPO Relationships

Comparing forms of cooperation—even in the same policy area—is very complex; there is little uniformity in these relationships, and they can develop in a contradictory fashion (Bode & Brandsen, 2014; Szeili & Zimmer, 2017). Coston's model of government–NPO relationships helps us classify these specific interactions by taking into account "government's resistance or acceptance of institutional pluralism, government NPO linkage, relative power relationship, degree of formality, favourability of government policy vis-a-vis NPO, and other type-specific characteristics" (Coston, 1998, 360). We will primarily be concerned with the models on the right side of Coston's relationship scale (as seen in Figure 1), as Germany's history reveals an acceptance of institutional pluralism or "welfare pluralism" as noted by Szeili & Zimmer (2017, 19). On this side of the scale, the relationships are increasingly based upon competitive advantage and involve the sharing of resources ranging from grants/contracts to the coordination of voluntary labour (Coston, 1998). The different relationship models depend upon the government's tolerance of the specific social organisation's influence and autonomy, combined with that organisation's willingness or ability to enter into formal relationships with government (Coston, 1998).

Specifically, we will use six of Coston's relationship models as presented in Figure 1. On the side of the scale where less institutional pluralism is accepted, the relationship types are competition, contracting and third-party government, which operate on a scale from informal to formal. Competition is related to government resistance to institutional pluralism, such that social organisations are critical of the government and are seen as competitors for local power. As regards contracting, social organisations provide services on behalf of the government, but they are allowed little input into the design of those services. The most formal of the three, third-party government, is similar to contracting, but in this relationship type social organisations have more autonomy in the use of public funds and public authority (Coston, 1998).

On the side where more institutional pluralism is accepted, the relationships feature cooperation, complementarity and collaboration, again with each having a different level of formality. Cooperation involves a more informal relationship defined by an unconstrained form of coexistence be-

tween the social organisation and government, with the possible duplica-
tion of services and free flow of information. Complementarity is based
upon mutual respect between government and social organisations, where
the competitive advantages in service provision offered by organisations
are combined with the "government's advantages in resource generation
and democratic priority setting." (Coston, 1998, 371). Collaboration, in
which the government and social organisations share the responsibility for
services and their operation, is more formalised; collaboration often results
in the formation of service networks that include multiple actors.

Figure 1: Coston's Model of Government–NPO Relationships (Coston, 1998)

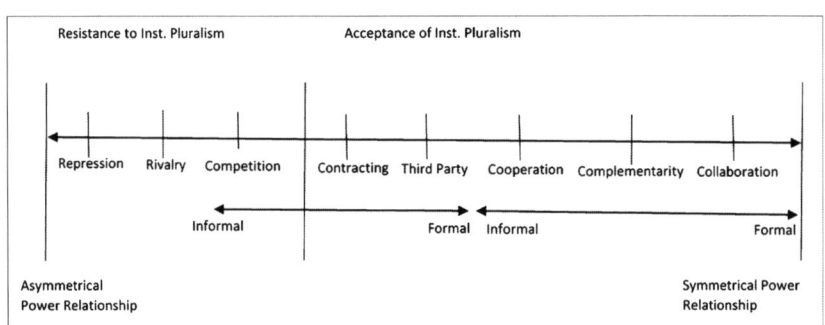

3 Overview of Cases

In the following, we will present the case studies conducted as part of the
LoGoSO project using the aforementioned theoretical framework. After
describing the selection criteria for the cases and the data collection
method, we will give an overview of the cases and highlight the project-
specific relationship models present in the study. Afterwards, two case
studies will be presented in detail.

3.1 Methods

This paper draws on nine case studies that were conducted as part of the
LoGoSO project (2016–2019). A detailed description of the case selection
methodology for the LoGoSO project can be found in the methods section
of the introduction to this volume. The German case studies were under-
taken in the cities of Berlin and Cologne in summer 2018. Eight of the case

studies present NPOs engaged in successful cooperation with local governments in the field of social services for refugees. Cooperation was considered successful if the NPO had existed for several years, engaged in diverse networks, and had stable funding and staff. A ninth case was chosen as an example of an 'unsuccessful case'. Furthermore, in line with the project's research interest, NPOs were identified that meet the following criteria:

- They all provide social services but operate in different policy areas, namely housing, education, employment and social assistance;
- at least one organisation was a newly established grassroots organisation, while at least one other was a member of a traditional German Welfare Association;
- at least one organisation was involved in policymaking; and
- at least one organisation emerged in response to an increase in migration with a focus on service provision.

Data for these case studies was collected by a review of local media reports and policy documents as well as qualitative expert interviews. All in all, 48 interviews were conducted with 22 government officials, 22 NPO representatives and 4 beneficiaries of services. The interviews were transcribed and, together with all the materials collected, were examined through qualitative content analysis, filtering information according to ex-ante fixed analytical categories (Gläser & Laudel, 2010). If necessary, the ex-ante fixed analytical categories were supplemented by inductive categories (Gläser & Laudel, 2010; Kaiser, 2014). The analysis was supported by MAXQDA software.

The analysis focuses on the relationships between the NPOs and actors from the public sphere in the field of refugee integration. We take a public administration perspective and refer to the aforementioned third-party government, network governance and relationship models to analyse the types of cooperation occurring in these two cities in Germany.

3.2 Summary of Cases

NPOs play a critical role in local refugee and integration policy in Germany (Szeili & Zimmer, 2017; Zimmer & Grabbe 2020). The data in this study shows that NPOs are key players in each of the following policy areas: education, housing, vulnerable groups and employment. Further, each of the case studies reveals elements of third-party government and network governance to varying degrees.

Aspects of third-party government are visible as all organisations provide services to refugees—a target group which has not been sufficiently covered by the market or public programmes so far. For this reason, several of the NPOs under study were newly established or were extending their existing service portfolio in reaction to the arrival of refugees in recent years. In the majority of cases (with the exception of *Be an Angel*), the government had begun to acknowledge the work of the NPOs, enter into contractual relationships with them or provide other support measures. At the same time, all cases show elements of network governance. The models range from formal networks established exclusively to provide housing or labour market access for refugees to more informal networks like working groups and round tables that allow the NPOs to bring their policy ideas directly to local government. Finally, all organisations were involved in networks with other NPOs or profit-oriented actors, be it the Free Welfare Associations or business associations.

Table 1 presents a summary comparison of all nine cases in the study. The cases are in order of how they align with Coston's (1998) government–NPO relationship model. Figure 2 shows where each case falls along the continuum.

Table 1 highlights a couple of interesting points in comparing these cases. Overall, 18 organisations are represented by these nine case studies. Only half of these organisations are members of larger established Welfare Associations. This is surprising considering the long prominence of Germany's Welfare Associations in all areas of service provision (Zimmer & Grabbe 2020).

In looking at the cooperative relationships by policy area, we see that, with the exception of employment, there is no consistency in the type of cooperative relationship by policy area. As previously mentioned, migration is a new policy area for local government. Employment is regulated at the federal level, which provides consistency between cities. The other important refugee integration services, such as housing and counselling, represent local-level policies (Szeili & Zimmer, 2017), which explains why the type of relationships in the same policy areas differ between the cities. Housing is an example of this: *Auszugsmanagement* in Cologne is a formal network model that is publicly funded and has strong connections to government (Grabbe, 2020c), whereas *Refugio* in Berlin is funded by the Berliner Stadtmission's general funds and is coordinated through informal case-by-case cooperation in response to the needs of individual refugees (Gluns, 2020b). The situation is similar for education; only in this policy area the cooperation is more formal in Berlin than in Cologne. In Berlin, *Kein Abseits!* has a mix of public and private funding and has formal cooperative relationships with schools, refugee accommodation and other government agencies (Schönert, 2020). In Cologne, *HOPE* has mostly private funding, and the cooperative efforts are informal and conducted on a case-by-case basis (Grabbe, 2020a).

Additionally, it might be expected that projects run by newer organisations would exist only at the lower end of Coston's 'acceptance of institutional pluralism scale', but this isn't strictly the case. *Kein Abseits!* is an example of an organisation, founded in the preceding decade, that maintains a large amount of autonomy and has developed strong connections with government (Schönert, 2020). It is possible that the early engagement of *Kein Abseits!* with local networks and their interest in policy development at the local, regional, national and European levels may have contributed to their ability to successfully enter into the local welfare structures. It is interesting to consider and compare this case to *Be an Angel*, the 'unsuccessful case' in this study. *Be an Angel*, which was founded four years after Kein Abseits!, has not managed to make inroads into the local welfare structure. It is possible that their sole focus on service provision does not produce the strategies needed to become a networked part of the local service landscape. It was also observed that *Be an Angel* has been very critical of government refugee service provision in Berlin (Gluns, 2020a). However, among these cases, *Be an Angel* is not the only organisation that advocates strongly for refugees, and, therefore, this quality in itself does not fully explain its lack of success in developing a cooperative relationship with local government. In fact, older organisations like the Refugee Counsel in Cologne started off in opposition to government but evolved into an autonomous organisation with high connectedness to local government; in fact, the *Auszugsmanagement* project is a collaboration in the form of a formal network that was initiated by *The Refugee Council* (Grabbe, 2020c).

Table 1: Summary of German LoGoSO case studies

Project/ Case Study	Organisa- tion(s)	Policy Area	Welfare Assoc. Member	Project Re- lationship Type	Cooperation: Funding & Services
Be an Angel (Berlin)	Be an Angel e.V.	Varied	No	Competition	Only private funding Informal: case-by-case contact to address indi- vidual needs
AWO Wom- en's Coun- selling Cen- ter (Berlin)	AWO Berlin District Associ- ation South- east	Vulnerable Groups (women)	Yes	Contracting	Only public funding via contracts Informal: case-by-case contact to address indi- vidual needs
Kein Ab- seits! (Berlin)	Kein Abseits! e.V.	Education	No	Third-Party Government	Mix of private and pub- lic funding Formal: cooperation with schools and public agencies
Refugio e.V. (Berlin)	Berliner Stadt- mission	Housing	Yes	Cooperation	Funded by Stadtmission general funds Informal: case-by-case contact to address indi- vidual needs
HOPE (Cologne)	Rheinflanke gGmbH (CG)	Education	Yes	Cooperation	Mostly private funding Informal: case-by-case contact to address indi- vidual needs
Agisra e.V. (Cologne)	Agisra e.V.	Vulnerable groups (women)	Yes	Comple- mentarity	Public funding via ad- ministrative grants Informal: case-by-case contact to address indi- vidual needs
Bridge e.V. (Berlin)	1 agency and 5 organisations	Employment	1 of 5	Collabora- tion, initiat- ed by gov- ernment	Only public funding via contracts Formal: network model
Auszugsma- nagement (Cologne)	1 agency and 3 organisations	Housing	2 of 3	Collabora- tion, initiat- ed by social organisation	Only public funding via contracts Formal: network model
Chance+ Network Refugees and Em- ployment (Cologne)	1 agency and 3 organisations	Employment	2 of 3	Collabora- tion, initiat- ed by gov- ernment	Only public funding via contracts Formal: network model

Figure 2: Adapted from Coston's Model of Government–NPO Relationships (Coston, 1998)

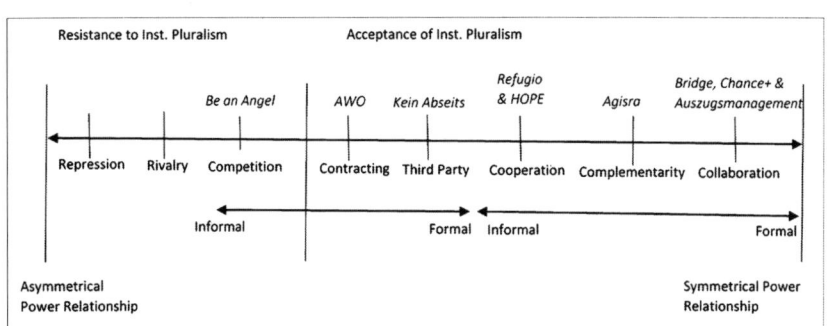

4 Representative Cases

To underscore the prevalence of third-party government and network governance models, we have selected two cases that represent the most formal examples of these models of cooperation found in this study. The selected cases also represent both cities:

- Integration by Education—*Kein Abseits! e.V.* in Berlin (Schönert, 2020)
- Employment—*Chance+ Network Refugees and Employment* in Cologne (Grabbe 2020b)

4.1 Kein Abseits!

4.1.1 Organisation Description

Kein Abseits! is an association founded in 2011 that promotes child and youth welfare, sports and active citizenship mainly in the Reinickendorf District of Berlin. *Kein Abseits!* translates directly to 'no offsides,' which is both a soccer reference and a nod to the organisation's mission to foster integration and not leave young people on the outskirts of society. The project is particularly focused on children and adolescents who have single parents, many siblings, parents with little education, few financial resources or a migration/refugee background. Many children in Berlin grow up with these risk factors, which impact their ability to succeed in the educational system and labour market and subsequently lead to poverty and social deprivation in whole neighbourhoods and quarters. *Kein Abseits!* is one of the few organisations offering measures to prevent this structural decline. The mission of the organisation grew out of the experiences of the two co-founders, who are themselves children of migrant guest workers.

Service provision by *Kein Abseits!* has a threefold approach: (1) sports and experiences that offer exercise; (2) social network building that is easily accessible to marginalised young people, and it involves 1-to-1 mentoring that pairs children aged 9 to 13 with university students in order for them to engage in educational, cultural and social activities; and (3) occupational exploration offered by adult professionals to help children explore career paths, opportunities and interests. The success of this approach has been recognised with awards from the Alliance for Democracy and Tolerance, the City of Berlin, the Senate Department of the Interior and Sports, Trade Union Education and Science Berlin, and the Robert-Bosch Foundation.

The sharp increase in refugees arriving in Berlin in 2015 led *Kein Abseits!* to develop specific programming to serve migrant children. The project "Heimspiel" (home play) was started in 2014 to serve girls living in refugee accommodation in Berlin-Reinickendorf. Since then, those services have been integrated into *Kein Abseits!*'s regular offers in order to strengthen the organisation's inclusive philosophy. However, migrants and refugees remain a central part of the service population.

Kein Abseits! is registered as a non-profit association according to the German Fiscal Code (Abgabenordnung). Its governance consists of a three-person executive board responsible for the association's activities, supervising its management, monitoring financial issues, protecting children and coordinating its members. There are four fields of operations: mentoring, pedagogical management, sports & adventure, and management. Management is focused on planning, strategy, finances, projects, human resources and public relations. Altogether, the association has around 20 members, most of whom are engaged as executive board members, managers and supervisors, self-employed trainers or volunteers.

Like many newly formed independent associations, *Kein Abseits!* is highly dependent on private funding. In 2016, 85% of its funding came from grants, donations and revenues and only 15% came from public sources. Additionally, the majority of funding takes the form of fixed-term (1 to 3 years) project funds, which makes long-term planning challenging. *Kein Abseits!* has been increasingly successful in securing public funds. In 2017, the proportion of its revenue from public sources increased to 30%. This success has a lot to do with the association's skill in connecting to local welfare networks (Schönert, 2020).

4.1.2 *Interest in Cooperation*

Kein Abseits! has had a clear interest in cooperating with the government from the very beginning. This is exhibited by the association's efforts to build networks and impact policy beyond its specific project interactions at the district level in Berlin. This interest may be what led *Kein Abseits!* to swiftly become part of the established welfare structure in Berlin (even if they are still a small player).

In Germany, big welfare providers have the advantage of long engagement at the local level, which leads to the largest share of public funding. They have the infrastructure to offer services at short notice and cope with complex and time-consuming administrative processes. Even without these advantages, *Kein Abseits!* became an established player at the local level due to its strategic efforts to engage with government and other service providers. It is therefore notable that *Kein Abseits!* is not a member of one of Germany's Welfare Associations.

A representative of the youth office described *Kein Abseits!* as "innovative and research-oriented in the development of their services" (Schönert, 2020). From the start, staff regularly attended network meetings in the district and worked flexibly and effectively with other service providers. *Kein Abseits!* has also shown itself to be a catalyst for new initiatives that extend beyond the day-to-day services that they offer. At the local level, they started the Working Group Refuge and Asylum (AG Asyl und Flucht)—a biannual meeting of field migration and integration professionals that now meets at the Refugee Coordination and the Youth Office of Reinickendorf.

Kein Abseits!'s initiatives extend beyond Reinickendorf. They co-founded the "Netzwerk Kinderpatenschaften" (network of child sponsorship)—a network of 36 social organisations which offer mentoring services in Berlin. The network exists to share knowledge, collectively advocate to impact the city's social agenda and organise mentorship services across Berlin. They even coordinate efforts to apply for funding to increase the likelihood of success. The network is also engaged at the European level. It initiated and co-led the European Mentoring & Befriending Exchange Program in 2014 and is often an organiser for the European Mentoring Summit and a member of the European Center of Evidence-Based Mentoring (ECEB) (Schönert, 2020).

4.1.3 Project Cooperation—Third-Party Government

The interests and ambitions of *Kein Abseits!* extend beyond the local level, as noted above, but their project-level cooperation with local government is at the centre of their service provision. Their cooperative engagement in the Reinickendorf district of Berlin is best described as third-party government. In this instance, government policy towards cooperative engagement is contingent on its specific relationship with the association. As a newer organisation, *Kein Abseits!* was able to become an important player in the established social welfare structure, which is often monopolised by the established welfare organisations. For one, it engages in resource sharing in the form of tax-exempt status and public funding, but *Kein Abseits!* is also able to maintain autonomy when it comes to its use of funds and influence over the social agenda. This is partially related to its strategic positioning in the local welfare networks and the fact that it brings resources like volunteers and private funds into the service mix.

In Coston's model, third-party government is the most formal of the relationships on the weaker side of the 'acceptance of institutional pluralism scale'. *Kein Abseits!* engages in formal cooperative engagement with the government and did so even before it had access to public funding. It began its cooperation with local schools and later connected with refugee accommodation, where it offered sports and mentoring services. From the start, it participated in "Kiez Runden" (Quarter-Meetings) to get involved in the local network. These meetings, the most important networks for local service provision, are part of the Sozialgesetzbuch (SGB; Social Code Book) and run by the Youth Office. Thanks to their consistent participation, *Kein Abseits!* became an officially recognised provider of children and youth welfare services (Träger der freien Kinder- und Jugendhilfe), making them eligible for public funds from the Youth Office (Schönert, 2020).

As previously mentioned, *Kein Abseits!* has had some success securing public funding. It doubled the proportion of public funds in its budget from 2016 to 2017. However, securing this funding has been challenging and has not led to long-term financial sustainability. Combining efforts with other members of "Netzwerk Kinderpatenschaften", it received funding from the Federal Ministry for Education and Research (BMBF) in 2012 and later in 2016 from the Senate Department of Education, Youth and Family for the project "1 zu 1 Flüchtlingspatenschaften" (1-to-1 refugee mentoring). When funding became available through Berlin's Master Plan for Integration and Security (Gluns, 2018b), representatives of the Youth Office immediately thought of *Kein Abseits!*, as they have "a portfolio that neither the Youth Office nor other providers in the district could offer and that is innovative and effective" (Schönert, 2020). However, when it comes to funding, its opportunities are limited. Even though *Kein Abseits!* is an integrated member of the social welfare network and is trusted and respected by the Youth Office, the Youth Office has very little flexible funding that is not already allocated to more established organisations. The extra funds made available by the Master Plan enabled *Kein Abseits!* to get a foot in the door, but its year-to-year funding isn't guaranteed in the future. At the time that Schönert (2020) wrote the case study, the association was at a crossroads of trying to figure out how to sustain services in the long run amidst these constraints.

4.2 *Chance+ Network for Refugees and Employment*

4.2.1 *Organisation Description*

Chance+ Network for Refugees and Employment is a network that supports refugee labour market integration and includes one government agency and three social organisations in the city of Cologne. The government agency that staffs the network coordinator is Cologne Job Center (Jobcenter Köln). The social organisations engaged in Cologne are IN VIA Catholic Association for Girls' and Women's Social Work (IN VIA Katholischer Verband für Mädchen- und Frauensozialarbeit), The Caritas Association of the City of Cologne (Cartiasverband für die Stadt Köln), and International Union (Internationaler Bund). Each of these network members are autonomous organisations that have long histories of service provision and engagement in workplace integration in Cologne. To give a clear picture of how this network functions, this section will first give a short description of each network member and then describe why the network was chosen as the preferred form of governance in this case.

Cologne Job Center is legislated by The Federal Ministry for Labour and Social Affairs (Bundesministerium für Arbeit und Soziales/BMAS) and administered by the Federal Employment Agency (Bundesagentur für Arbeit) in cooperation with the city of Cologne (Gluns, 2018b). The Job Center manages long-term unemployment benefits (UBII) and provides labour market support in the form of education and training, counselling and placement, self-employed services and counselling for specific target groups including refugees. Cologne Job Center employs 1500 staff but no volunteers and is fully funded by the city and the federal government (Gluns, 2018b).

IN VIA Catholic Association for Girls' and Women's Social Work was founded in 1898 by wealthy Catholic women to help women and girls in need make a living. What started off as services to help women and girls from rural areas who came to Cologne for work expanded into assistance for female Spanish guest workers in the 1960s and later child and youth welfare for migrant children. Currently, IN VIA runs over 6 projects across Cologne that serve children and adolesecents regardless of their gender, origin or belief. Specific services for refugees range from travel support and first orientation, accommodation for unaccompanied minors and counselling. *Chance+* is not IN VIA's only cooperative effort to integrate refugees into the labour market; it also provides language tutoring and education to refugees as part of the federal programme "Quality is no coincidence—New Standards for Refugee Work" (Qualität ist kein Zufall – Neue Standards für die Flüchtlingsarbeit) and helps refugees get recognised for previously acquired qualifications through the Job Center programme "KompAS" (IN VIA 2017). IN VIA employs 616 staff and 162 volunteers, and its budget consists of 59% public and 31% private funding.

The Caritas Association of the City of Cologne was founded in 1915 to unite Catholic social service organisations that were attempting to alleviate hardships caused by the First World War (Caritasverband für die Stadt Köln e.V., 2016). While Caritas only provided support to other organisations in its early years, it began providing services like childcare and retirement homes after the Second World War. Similarly to IN VIA, Caritas began serving guest worker migrants in the 1960s. Today, Caritas provides a wide array of services to migrants, children, the disabled and the elderly at over 80 facilities in Cologne. Services targeted to refugees include group accommodation and help finding housing, legal counselling, trauma care and language education. In addition to *Chance+*, Caritas matches refugees with mentors to help them search for employment through the programme "New Neighbours Initiative" (Aktion Neue Nachbarn) and runs 6-week job market orientation courses and 6-week internships for refugees under 35 who are asylum seekers or are tolerated by the state. Caritas employs 1,765 staff and 1,630 volunteers, and the majority of its funding comes from service charges (76%), a small portion derives from public funds (11%), while the rest is provided by the Church.

International Union was founded in 1945 to assist young people who were homeless and unemployed in Tübingen, many of whom lacked an education due to the Second World War. Since then, the organisation has significantly expanded its services, target groups and geographic spread. Today, the Union provides education and training to help people of all ages who are living in difficult circumstances. It is active in 300 locations all over Germany. In Cologne, the Union works primarily in schools and training centres. It offers services such as mobile social work, job counselling and training, general education, childcare and housing for the disabled and homeless. In addition to *Chance+*, International Union funds the programme "Prospects for Female Refugees" (Perspektiven für weibliche Flüchtlinge/PERF w), which provides language support and information about the German labour market to female asylum seekers and recognised refugees. Germany-wide, the organisation employs 14,000 staff, and the majority of its funding is public (80%), with fees, insurance payments and donations making up the balance (Grabbe, 2020b).

4.2.2 Interest in Cooperation

The institutional interest in cooperation among the three social organisations engaged in *Chance+ Cologne* is not all the same. Caritas has a long history of cooperation on both policy development and implementation, while the International Union and IN VIA have mostly been engaged in service provision and implementation. Caritas cooperates with multiple public authorities and private organisations. Additionally, it engages in public policymaking as a member of the Round Table of Refugee Issues Cologne (Runder Tisch für Flüchtlingsfragen Köln) and as part of a campaign and commission to grant refugees with exceptional leave permanent residency permits in Cologne.

The other two organisations do not engage directly in policymaking; instead, they have a significant history of cooperative service provision in conjunction with other public and private entities at the local, national and international levels. Both organisations are also a part of Quality Community Professional Education Cologne (Qualitätsgemeinschaft Berufliche Bildung Köln), which ensures quality service for organisations providing vocational training. IN VIA is also one of five Caritas members and, as such, is able to benefit from Caritas's public policy work without having to directly engage in advocacy.

As a network, *Chance+* is focused on service provision to improve the lives of refugees with the legal status of exceptional leave to remain. It does not directly engage in policymaking; instead, it operates as a silent player. Since the Job Center is a member of the network and employs the coordinator, the network cannot advocate on behalf of refugees (Grabbe, 2020b).

4.2.3 Project Cooperation—Network Governance

The *Chance+* network is a good illustration of networked governance and demonstrates why the network approach was chosen as the governance form of choice.

First of all, as expected in the public sector, the network was initiated from the top down. It was established by Germany's national government with the goal of improving job market integration for targeted groups, among them asylum seekers, recognised refugees and those with an exceptional leave to remain ('tolerated') who are served by the programme "Integration of Asylum Seekers and Refugees" (Integration von Asylsuchenden und Flüchtlingen/IvAF) (BMAS, 2017). This, however, does not include refugees who are excluded from the labour market because they come from places that are considered 'safe countries of origin' (Gluns, 2018).

In order to participate, regions must put together a network of providers, one that preferably includes private partners like NPOs and businesses, to provide job counselling and placement, network building, and access to expert knowledge. These networks apply to the Federal Ministry for competitive funding, 50% of which is provided by the European Social Fund (ESF), 40% by the Federal Ministry for Labour and Social Affairs (Bundesministerium für Arbeit und Soziales), and 10% by the network partners themselves (BMAS, 2017). *Chance+* is one of 41 IvAF networks across the country.

Chance+ is based upon two previous employment networks that focused on people without permanent residency permits who are therefore ineligible for regular services provided at job centres. The previous networks were the KNFA (Kölner Netzwerk Flüchtlinge und Arbeit/Cologne Network for Refugees and Labour) and Colourful into the Future (Bunt in die Zukunft). These 'tolerated' migrants are a major focus of *Chance+*, and the network operates under the idea that employment offers refugees who lack residency the possibility of a guaranteed right to stay. All three NPOs were engaged in one or both of these previous networks, and the KNFA was coordinated by a previous form of the Job Center. Therefore, the network partners have a long history of frequently exchanging knowledge, ideas and information, which has fostered strong ties between them.

Second, with regard to the different network forms identified by Provan and Kenis (2007, 233), it can be said that the governance of the network is not shared but executed by a lead organisation. The role of the lead organisation is conducted by the network coordinator, who is employed by the Job Center. The coordinator is responsible for performing administration related to the network, organising monthly meetings, and taking on a steering role when the network interacts with external partners. It is advantageous for the network that the coordinator is employed by the Job Center, as it creates a strong connection to local government; the Job Center is a joint facility of the Federal Employment Agency and the city of Cologne. Job Center employees see *Chance+* as a supplemental service that they are happy to utilise, and the Job Center provides *Chance+* with a technical infrastructure to draw upon. The network also participates in internal monthly meetings held by the Job Center. Additionally, all network partners cooperate with public institutions outside the Job Center, in particular the immigration authority, housing authority and the local integration centres. This includes knowledge sharing via training to other public and private entities including politicians, administration officials and those from business and civil society.

Third, it is beneficial for the participant organisations to follow a network model because they all share a common goal: integrating refugees into the local labour market. However, as services for refugees are very specific and there is plenty of uncertainty created by a frequently changing legal environment (Bogumil et al., 2006), this goal is difficult to achieve. Thus, they have realised that they are likely to be more successful if they combine their various areas of expertise and resources.

Caritas, IN VIA and International Union offer the comparative advantages of long histories working in labour market integration, connection to migrant communities and supplemental service offers that can improve overall outcomes for refugees. All organisations are currently involved in numerous labour market or educational programmes for refugees. So, with the exception of the work of the coordinator, the tasks accomplished by network partners overlap. Each organisation provides counselling, placement and training. However, this is balanced by each organisation's different expertise and their offers of additional refugee-focused services. Caritas employs two *Chance+* staff who provide individual counselling, job placement and placement in training programmes offered by third parties. Caritas's refugee services that complement *Chance+* include social counselling for victims of trauma, mentoring, informational events, and counselling and training for employers working in the labour market integration of refugees. As part of *Chance+*, IN VIA employs two staff and offers individual counselling, job placement, application training and referral to language courses, and contracts directly with businesses to provide work experience and job orientation to refugees. IN VIA also assists businesses with legal matters pertaining to refugee integration and guides refugees during their first few weeks of employment. International Union employs two *Chance+* staff and provides counselling and job placement like the other partner organisations, but its major strength is job orientation and in-house training opportunities.

A fourth aspect of the network approach is that, contrary to hierarchical forms of governance, network partners maintain their autonomy. This becomes clear when analysing the extent to which the network as a whole, and the individual organisations, advocate for the rights of refugees. While the network must maintain a more moderate role in advocacy efforts on behalf of 'tolerated' refugees, the individual social organisations maintain their autonomy in this area and are free to participate in political forums and round tables focused on these issues. As mentioned previously, Caritas is particularly engaged in public policy advocacy on behalf of refugees and it does not appear to have impacted its engagement as part of *Chance+* or its other cooperative arrangements. Further, as long as partners stay within contract guidelines, they are free to implement *Chance+* how they see fit and select the desired personnel. The coordinator of the network is very open to new ideas and the thematic priorities of the network organisations.

In terms of the number of participants it has integrated into the labour market, *Chance+* has been very successful. Since 2015, more than 50% of *Chance+* participants have been integrated into the labour market. Measures of the overall IvAF-programme show a rate of 26% of participants provided with education, vocational training or work. It appears to be a particular strength of *Chance+* that the coordinator for the network is employed by the Job Center, which is not the case with other IvAF networks. This provides the network with particularly good connections to the Job Center and other local public authorities. Furthermore, the network's success rests in its ability to have services provided by social organisations that extend beyond legal and job counselling and include social counselling, mentoring and job market education. (Grabbe, 2020b)

While *Chance+* has grown into a network where the partners have great trust in one another and participant placements are above the national average, the project is not without its challenges. The highly bureaucratic nature of the federal programme creates the need for staff to manage time-consuming administrative processes, and partners feel that the provision of 1.5 full time-equivalent staff is not sufficient to comply with administrative requirements while also putting sufficient time into counselling participants. Further, the fact that this is a time-constrained project makes it difficult to retain staff who have the experience and personal connections that are important to the success of the network. Finally, *Chance+* is no longer seen as the primary expert on asylum and labour laws or the main provider of refugee labour market integration services in Cologne (Gluns, 2018a).

The increase in other projects has created a complicated structure in Cologne, which makes it difficult for refugees to navigate and has diluted the network's influence on policy (Grabbe, 2020b).

5 Conclusion

This paper investigates models of cooperation between the government and non-profit organisations in the policy area of migration in Germany from a public administration research perspective. The LoGoSO case studies in Cologne and Berlin present a range of cooperative models that exist between the government and NPOs. Overall, third-party government and network governance are the preferred forms of interaction. Third-party government can be observed as the NPOs in this study either were founded in reaction to the arrival of a large number of migrants in recent years or have expanded their existing service portfolio. Local government sought to cooperate with these NPOs by providing contracts, support funding and infrastructure instead of setting up its own programmes and services. At the same time, all the cases show elements of network governance. These networks range from formal networks coordinated by local government actors to improve labour market access for refugees to more informal types of networks like round tables or working groups where NPOs have the opportunity to voice their ideas and concerns related to policymakers.

In studying the factors that influence this cooperation, the LoGoSO case studies reveal that the cooperative relationships are not as dependent on the established German social welfare associations as might be expected. Half of the organisations represented in the study are not members of an association. There is also little alignment between the cooperative relationship and policy areas. Employment is the only field that has the same model in both cities, which makes sense as labour market integration is federal policy in Germany. In this field, the federal government initiated local networks to integrate refugees into the labour market. In contrast, the policy areas of housing, social assistance and education are local-level policies, and, therefore, cooperation models differ between the cities in this respect. They are influenced by local funding opportunities and traditions of cooperation. Further, the age of the organisation seems to have little influence on the degree of formality of the cooperation, as relatively young organisations were able to develop strong ties to the local administration authorities while, at the same time, staying autonomous. The cases also demonstrate that early involvement in local networks and a great extent of advocacy work on the local, federal and European levels can help organisations draw the attention of policymakers to them and become integrated into the local infrastructure of service provision.

References

Bode, Ingo and Brandsen, Taco (2014). "State–third Sector Partnerships: A short overview of key issues in the debate", *Public Management Review*, 16:8, 1055–1066, online available at: https://doi.org/10.1080/14719037.2014.957344.

Bogumil, Jörg and Werner Jann, Frank Nullmeier, Frank (eds.) (2006). *Politik und Verwaltung. Politische Vierteljahresschrift* (special edition, vol. 37).

Coston, Jennifer M. (1998). "A Model and Typology of Government-NPO Relationships", *Nonprofit and Voluntary Sector Quarterly*, 27(3), 358–382, online available at: https://doi.org/10.1177/0899764098273006.

Dossi, Samuele (2017). *Cities and the European Union: Mechanisms and Modes of Europeanisation*. Colchester: European Consortium for Political Research.

Gläser, Jochen and Grit Laudel (2010). *Experteninterviews und qualitative Inhal.tsanalyse als Instrumente rekonstruierender Untersuchungen*(4. Auflage). Lehrbuch. Wiesbaden: VS Verlag, online available at: http://d-nb.info/1002141753/04.

Gluns, Danielle (2020a). "A case of unsuccessful co-operation? – Be an Angel e.V.", *LoGoSO Research Papers*, No. 16, online available at: https://refubium.fu-berlin.de/handle/fub188/26796.

Gluns, Danielle (2020b). "Social Assistance and Housing – The Refugio Berlin", *LoGoSO Research Papers*, No. 14, online available at: https://refubium.fu-berlin.de/handle/fub188/26794.

Gluns, Danielle (2018a). "Labour Market Policy and Integration in Germany", *LoGoSO Research Papers*, Nr. 2. online available at: https://refubium.fu-berlin.de/handle/fub188/21957.

Gluns, Danielle (2018b). "Refugee Integration Policy and Public Administration in Berlin, *LoGoSO Research Papers*, No. 6., online available at: https://refubium.fu-berlin.de/handle/fub188/22193.

Grabbe, Christina (2020a). "Education – RheinFlanke: HOPE", *LoGoSO Research Papers*, No. 20, online available at: https://refubium.fu-berlin.de/handle/fub188/26799.

Grabbe, Christina (2020b). "Employment – Chance+. Network Refugees and Employment", *LoGoSO Research Papers*, No. 19, online available at: https://refubium.fu-berlin.de/handle/fub188/26798.

Grabbe, Christina (2020c). "Social Assistance and Housing – Auszugsmanagement", *LoGoSO Research Papers*, No. 18, online available at: https://refubium.fu-berlin.de/handle/fub188/26793.

Hartley, Jean (2005). "Innovation in Governance and Public Services: Past and Present", *Public Money and Management*, 25:1, 27–34.

Howlett, Michael and Anka Kekez, Ora-Orn Poocharoen (2017). "Understanding Co-Production as a Policy Tool: Integrating New Public Governance and Comparative Policy Theory", *Journal of Comparative Policy Analysis: Research and Practice*, 19:5, 487–501, online: https://doi.org/10.1080/13876988.2017.1287445.

Jones, Candace and William S. Hesterly, Stephen P. Borgatti (1997). "A General Theory of Network Governance: Exchange Conditions and Social Mechanisms", *The Academy of Management Review*, 22, 911–945.

Kaiser, Robert (2014). *Qualitative Experteninterviews: Konzeptionelle Grundlagen und praktische Durchführung*. Lehrbuch. Wiesbaden: Springer VS. Online: https://doi.org/10.1007/978-3-658-02479-6.

Meyer, Renate E. and Gerhard Hammerschmid (2006). "Changing Institutional Logics and Executive Identities: A Managerial Challenge to Public Administration in Austria", *American Behavioral Scientist*, 49, 1000–1014.

Osborn, Stephen P. (2006). "The New Public Governance?", *Public Management Review*, 8:3, 377–387.

Pestoff, Victor (2012). "Co-Production and Third Sector Social Services in Europe". In Victor Pestoff, Taco Brandsen, and Bram Verschuere (eds.). *New Public Governance, the Third Sector, and Co-Production*, New York, NY: Routledge, 13–34.

Pollitt, Christopher and Geert Bouckaert (2017). *Public Management Reform: A Comparative Analysis – Into the Age of Austerity* (4th edition). Oxford: Oxford University Press.

Polzer, Tobias (2016). *Von klassischer Verwaltung zu Public Governance. Rolle von Verwaltungsparadigmen in Reformen des öffentlichen Rechnungswesens*. Wiesbaden: Springer VS.

Provan, Keith G. and Patrick Kenis (2007). "Modes of Network Governance: Structure, Management, and Effectiveness", *Journal of Public Administration Research and Theory*, 18:2, 229–252, online available at: https://doi.org/10.1093/jopart/mum015.

Salamon, Lester M. (1995). *Partners in Public Service: Government-Nonprofit Relations in the Modern Welfare State*. Baltimore: The Johns Hopkins University Press.

Schnapp, Kai-Uwe (2006). "Comparative Public Administration". In Jörg Bogumil, Werner Jann and Frank Nullmeier, Frank (eds.). *Politik und Verwaltung. Politische Vierteljahresschrift*. (special edition, vol. 37).

Schönert, Caroline (2020). "Integration by Education – Kein Abseits! e.V.", *LoGoSO Research Papers*, No. 21, Berlin, online available at: https://refubium.fu-berlin.de/handle/fub188/26800.

Szeili, Judith and Annette Zimmer (2017). "Local Public Administration and Local Social Policy in Germany", *LoGoSo Research Report 2*, online available at: https://logoso-project.com/publications/.

Torfing, Jacob (2014). "Governance networks". In David Levi-Faur (ed.). *The Oxford Handbook of Governance* Oxford: Oxford University Press, 99–112.

Zimmer, Annette and Christina Grabbe (2020). "Models of Public Administration and the German Tradition of Subsidiarity", *LoGoSO Research Papers, No. 24*, online available at: https://refubium.fu-berlin.de/handle/fub188/26803.

Outsourcing and Networking: Similar Trends in Local State–NPO Cooperation in Germany and China

Katja Levy and Anja Ketels[1]

1 Introduction

Under the influence of New Public Management (NPM), cooperation between non-profit organisations (NPOs) and local governments has become a crucial part of modern governance[2] (Salamon 1995). Theories of the welfare state have often based explanations of NPO involvement in governance processes on some type of failure whereby local governments cannot provide sufficient social services which in turn induces social actors to step in and fill the gaps (see Salamon 1987, 33–36). Salamon (1987) took this discussion further and introduced a theory of voluntary failure to explain the importance of NPO-government cooperation. According to this theory, the government mobilises and supports the non-profit sector for partici-

---

1 The authors are grateful for the helpful comments by reviewers Mark Sidel and Christina Maags and the additional comments by other scholars on earlier versions of the paper at the ARNOVA annual conference in San Diego in November 2019 and at the annual meeting of the Working Group of Social Science Researchers on China (ASC) of the German Association for Asian Studies. An earlier version of this paper was published under the title "Outsourcing and networking: Common trends in local state–NPO cooperation in Germany and China" in the Working Paper Series of the LoGoSO Research Project, online available at: https://refubium.fu-berlin.de/handle/fub188/25894. This article was originally published in *Nonprofit Policy Forum* https://doi.org/10.1515/npf-2020-0005 (minor corrections have been made).
2 We understand governance in its "new" sense, namely "in that it focuses less on the state and its institutions and more on social practices and activities" (Bevir 2012, 1). As Salamon explains: "'new governance' [...] shifts the attention from hierarchic agencies to organisational networks. The defining characteristic of many of the most widely used and most rapidly expanding tools [...] is their indirect character, their establishment of interdependencies between public agencies and a host of third-party actors" (Salamon 2011, 1628). He further clarifies: "rather than seeing such collaboration as an aberration or a violation of appropriate administrative practice, moreover, the 'new governance' views it as a desirable byproduct of the important complementarities that exist among the sectors, complementarities that can be built upon to help solve public problems" (Salamon 2011, 1633).

pation in governance processes. NPOs support government provision of social services, while the government compensates for NPO shortcomings such as limited resources and inadequate distribution thereof (Salamon 1987, 36–42). In both Germany and China, this development and the associated debate have recently gained new momentum in response to the challenges of providing social services to migrants. At the peak of the current influx of refugees into Germany in 2015, approximately 890,000 asylum seekers[3] entered the country in one year and strained the capacities of local administrations (see Altrock and Kunze 2016). Civil society actors responded by developing new programs and showing high potential for engagement and innovation. In China, affluent cities face similar challenges in response to huge numbers of migrant workers arriving from poor rural areas (see Cai and Liu 2015). In 2018, a total of around 288 million migrant workers were counted in the country.[4] Local governments must develop new means of providing social services and integration opportunities for the new populations in their cities.[5] Administrations in both Germany and China are searching for solutions to these new challenges, and in both

---

3 Press release from the Federal Ministry of the Interior, 30 Sept. 2016, online available at http://www.bmi.bund.de/SharedDocs/Pressemitteilungen/DE/2016/09/asylsuchende-2015.html (last access: August 16, 2019).

4 National Bureau of Statistics of the Chinese government, 29 April 2019, online available at http://www.stats.gov.cn/tjsj/zxfb/201904/t20190429_1662268.html (last access: August 16, 2019).

5 In both Germany and China, the responsibility for providing social services to migrants lies with the local government. A working paper summarized this similarity as follows: "In Germany, the local government, i.e. the specific municipality and/or federal state, is in principle the first provider of social services to migrants. The municipality (*Kommune*) is the third administrative level in the hierarchy, below the federal government (*Bund*) and the federal states (*Bundesländer*). Municipalities, in turn, include various local administrative and territorial structures such as communities, districts (*Kreise*), cities associated with districts (*Kreisstädte*) and independent cities (*kreisfreie Städte*) (Szeili und Zimmer 2017, 2 f.). [...] In China, the term 'local government' refers to all levels below the central government, namely the provinces, prefectures, counties and villages (Ma, Fan and Shan 2017, 1). Local governments' social service provision for migrants is still very limited due to the household registration system. However, they do bear the responsibility of providing social services in their jurisdiction" (Levy 2020,7). In our analysis, we primarily refer to the administrative levels of the four sample cities: Guangzhou and Hangzhou both have the status of prefecture-level cities that are only subordinate to the province and the central government. Berlin is a city-state, i.e. a city that simultaneously has the federal status; and in Cologne, the unit of analysis is the municipal level, which is however influenced by the federal state of North-Rhine Westphalia.

countries civil society is stepping in and playing an increasingly important role in governance processes (see Hasmath and Hsu 2018; Freise and Zimmer 2019).

Based on the results of a three-year German-Chinese comparative research project, this article examines modes of state-society cooperation. Taking social services offered by societal actors to migrants in two Chinese and two German cities as case studies, we identify and analyse characteristics and underlying rationales of cooperation between local governments and NPOs.

Our decision to select cases in the two countries China and Germany and in the particular area of service provision for migrants requires an explanation. We chose the two countries because they are obviously very different. These clear differences in terms of political system, culture, history, geography, and economic system mean that similar findings regarding the modes of cooperation are more significant than they would be for two more similar countries.[6] In addition, resulting similarities in the governance processes cannot be attributed to similarities of the political system, culture, history, geography, and economic system exactly because of these differences. We chose services for migrants, because the influx of migrants coming to the cities and demanding services and integration posed similar challenges to the local governments in both countries in the period studied (2016–2019). As mentioned above, the burden of providing social services lies on the shoulders of these local governments, and they seek to share this responsibility with social organisations that often act as more or less equal partners who contribute their knowledge, skills and human resources to varying forms of cooperation.

The results of our qualitative field research in the two countries indicate similar cooperative trends. From a top-down perspective German and Chinese local governments show similar outsourcing modes, while from a bottom-up perspective NPOs show similar practices of network governance albeit in different settings and with different power relations. We argue that NPOs and local governments deploy similar strategies in their joint at-

---

6 Less for this article, but for the larger LoGoSO project it is also interesting to see that, at different points of time, the two countries have made similar experiences. Both countries have traditionally emphasized the central role of the family in providing social services, and their early ideas on social policy revolved around protecting workers, and later developed forms of corporatist state-social organisational relations. These developments have more recently been modified by neoliberal trends in public administration and the growing importance of commercial service providers.

tempt to tackle social problems, regardless of their political backgrounds. This research is based on first-hand observations on how social organisations provide services for migrants in Germany and China. By analysing cooperation modes pursued by NPOs and the state, this research contributes to the broader political science issue of governance.

In recent years, the question of how to integrate migrants has posed an exceptional challenge to local governments in China and Germany. The two countries have very different histories of migration. China has had relatively little immigration from foreigners but a brief and intense phase of internal migration, while Germany has a long history of immigrants from foreign countries with many fluctuations over past centuries (Ketels 2019, 7). This study focuses on recent migration trends in the two countries. China has seen intensified and more permanent internal migration over recent years. Huge numbers of people have moved from poor rural regions to affluent cities to improve their living conditions. The Chinese system does not recognise these migrants as full residents of their new destinations but rather considers them a floating population and refers to persons who stay in one location for only a limited amount of time. This floating population is usually not eligible for the household registration (hukou) at their destination which enables access to social services. Migrant workers moving to the Chinese industrial centres in search of better economic conditions for their families are the largest group within the floating population (Levy 2020, 2–4).

In Germany, the recent influx of large numbers of refugees from war-torn countries, such as Syria, Iran and Afghanistan, is the focus of this study. Since 2015, what is called the "refugee crisis" has dominated public debate, challenged the capacities of local administrations and triggered engagement by NPOs. Although there are different legal forms of asylum in Germany, because they entail similar rights for the persons in question all of these groups will be referred to as "refugees" in this paper. Most refugees are expected to stay in Germany for long periods of time, which makes their access to social services and integration a long-term political goal (Ketels 2019, 8; Levy 2020, 2–4).

The challenges involved in providing social services to the floating population in China and to refugees in Germany are similar in the sense that the migrants do not have full access to the regular social systems and that local administrations lack the resources and expertise to develop adequate solutions. In both countries, NPOs have responded to this challenge and showed exceptional readiness to develop assistance systems for migrants. Local administrations benefit from the NPOs' efforts and expertise and readily establish cooperation with them. Migration therefore provides an excellent policy field to explore modes of NPO-state cooperation.

The remaining parts of this article are structured as follows: The literature review in section 2 summarises previous research on state–NPO cooperation in Western, i.e. North American and European, societies and in China. We then introduce our data collection and analysis methods in section 3. In section 4 we develop the theoretical framework of outsourcing for the top-down perspective and networking for the bottom-up perspective of the analysis, which we then apply in section 5 to the qualitative content of nineteen cases of state–NPO cooperation. The concluding section summarises and discusses our results.

2 *State of the Art: State–NPO Cooperation Structures in China and Germany*

State–NPO cooperative relationships in China and in Germany come from very different backgrounds and contexts. In China, the authoritarian system and the Communist Party's exclusive claim to power determine practically every development, whereas Germany traditionally depends on a corporatist power-sharing system with the non-profit sector as the backbone of the welfare state. However, the two systems face similar challenges in providing social services, and current discussions on best practices in this field show parallels. Against the background of NPM,[7] the governments of both countries have developed ways of cooperating with NPOs to make use of the latter's productivity and expertise in providing social services.

Western research projects have taken several different approaches in explaining these cooperative relationships. Zimmer emphasises the markedly multifunctional nature of NPOs which makes them open to different types of cooperation, including with the state (Zimmer 2010, 201). Najam (2000) identifies four different possibilities for state–NPO cooperation based on institutional interests and preferences for policy ends and means, i.e. cooperative, confrontational, complementary or cooptative. Young

---

7 New Public Management (NPM) is an approach to making public services more market-based rather than hierarchically organised. It first developed in the UK and Australia during the 1980s and soon gained popularity all over the world. Christopher Hood summarizes the main ideas of NPM as follows: "Hands-on professional management in the public sector; explicit standards and measures of performance; greater emphasis on output controls; shift to a disaggregation of units in the public sector; stress on private-sector styles of management practice; stress on greater discipline and parsimony in resource use" (Hood 1991, 4f).

(2000) found that complementary, supplementary and adversarial relations between the state and non-profit sectors exist in different countries, but vary over time and relative dominance. For Salamon (1987), efficiency and effectiveness are the major drivers for government/third-sector partnerships (Zimmer 2010, 201). Finally, Salamon and Toepler combine "voluntary failure" and third-party government/new governance theory in their explanations for state and non-profit cooperation. Voluntary failure denotes the deficiencies of the NPOs themselves, which combine with the deficiencies of the market and the government and therefore enhance cooperation. In their view, typical deficiencies of NPOs are philanthropic insufficiency, philanthropic particularism, philanthropic paternalism, and philanthropic amateurism. New governance theory considers a broad range of government limitations with regard to solving social problems and complements the insights of NPM by emphasising not only internal management mechanisms in state bureaucracies but also the different instruments of state/non-profit cooperation. In particular, it seeks to utilise the special strengths of NPOs, such as their flexibility, their own institutional structures and their ability to tailor services to individual needs (Salamon and Toepler 2015, 2162 ff.).

As for China, the predominate (Western) explanation for the close relationship between the state and NPOs was the theory of corporatism. Originally, corporatism was used to explain a state-society relationship in which interest representation was organised top-down. Schmitter defined corporatism as "a system of interest representation in which the constituent units are organised into a limited number of singular, compulsory, non-competitive, hierarchically ordered and functionally differentiated categories, recognized or licensed (if not created) by the state and granted a deliberate representational monopoly within their respective categories in exchange for observing certain controls on their selection of leaders and articulation of demands and supports" (Schmitter 1974, 93 f.). Unger and Chan (1995) were among the first scholars to propose using this concept to explain the relationship between state and societal organisations in the People's Republic of China (PRC). In doing so, they emphasised that corporatism was applied as a way to organise societal sectors without direct state intervention. As they write: "within such corporatist framework, the state does not attempt to dominate directly. It leaves some degree of autonomy to the organisations within each of their respective spheres of operation. But to ensure that the compacts and agreements achieved at the top get implemented effectively, it demands that the organisations exercise some discipline and control over their own memberships" (Unger and Chan 1995, 30). The two scholars also distinguished social or liberal corporatism on the one hand, and authoritarian state corporatism on the other. While the former term is used for Western democracies in describing how the "leaders of the peak association are beholden to their memberships, not the state, and the state is not directly in a position to dictate the terms of agreement between sectors" (Unger and Chan 1995, 31), the latter term is reserved for authoritarian regimes like China "where the weight of decision-making power lies very heavily on the side of the state" (Unger and Chan 1995, 31). They emphasise that "[w]hat both ends of this corporatist spectrum hold in common is the notion that organised consensus and cooperation are needed, in contrast to the divisive competition and conflict entailed by pluralist interest-group models of organisation (Unger and Chan 1995, 32). The focus of this theoretical approach is interest representation and political steering of certain societal sectors via representative organisations of these sectors.

Corporatist approaches had great explanatory value for the situation in China in the 1980s and 1990s when "government-organised non-governmental organisations" (GONGOs), i.e. large organisations initiated either by the state or the Communist Party, such as the *China Children and Teenagers Fund*, the *Communist Youth League* and the *All-China Federation of Trade Unions*, were used as "conveyor belts" to transport Party policies down to the people and people's grievances up to the political decision makers.

However, today we find that many service organisations are neither state-organised nor consider interest representation to be their primary mission. In our sample, the Chinese organisations also generally take the legal form of *social service organisation* (社会服务机构 *shehui fuwu jigou*), which is not membership-based and therefore cannot function as representative of a certain societal sector. Instead, they offer services as a type of profession or business, even though they have to be registered by the state and in most cases work closely together with the authorities. This is why new theoretical approaches have arisen in research on the third sector in recent years, which try to capture and explain this shift and complement or even replace the corporatist approach. Jessica Teets, for example, has added the concept of consultative authoritarianism to this China-related set of explanations of state/non-profit cooperation. She showed how recentralisation and tax reform in favour of the central government have forced local governments to consider NPOs as alternative public service providers. Increased dependence on NPOs has made the government reluctant to take violent and extra-legal actions against them (Teets 2014). Further recent approaches include that of Hildebrandt (2013), who explained the Chinese state-society relationship as a form of codependency.

Levy and Pissler (2020) take a functional perspective and suggest viewing cooperation between the Chinese state and NPOs as a form of governance.

From a Chinese perspective, the country's economic and social development has required new development strategies for NPOs and more complex involvement by them in governance processes (Ma and Liao 2015). Jing (2015) shows that the Chinese government has responded to these new developments and challenges by intensifying its control strategies on the one hand and by starting to actively empower the development of NPOs on the other. In a similar vein, Kang and Han (2008) apply their "system of graduated controls" to analyse the extent to which state control depends on a given organisation's scope, its capacity to challenge the state, and its value to public services. Wang and Kang (2018) summarise a tightened reconfiguration of policy and power that commenced in the wake of the 18th party congress in 2012 and accompanies the reorientation from purely state-centred, economically oriented policy to more diverse and sustainable development policy, which in turn encompasses the increasing involvement of NPOs in state structures (Wang and Kang 2018, 1). Over the course of this development, the system of government service purchasing (GSP) from NPOs has gained momentum and the Chinese government has emphasised "fully recogniz[ing] the importance of GSP from social forces" (Wang and Snape 2018, 4).

In Germany, the neo-corporatist welfare state traditionally involves non-state actors in the provision of social services (Evers 2011). For decades, a limited number of umbrella organisations operated in close partnership with the government and enjoyed a privileged position in policymaking and access to funding (Zimmer 2010). Since the early 1990s, this position has changed and given way to a system in which NPOs must compete with for-profit social service providers (Freise and Zimmer 2019, 14). Freise and Zimmer (2019) argue that a new assessment of the German welfare state and the role of civil society is needed as the traditional welfare mix is currently at a crossroad defined by changing actor constellations, new social problems and new political strategies (Freise and Zimmer 2019, 395).

In summary, both Germany and China have a tradition of corporatist state–NPO relations, which, however, gave way to more diversified and market-driven cooperation models. This article contributes to the larger discussion on state-society cooperation, and more substantially to a more nuanced understanding of the characteristics and rationales of state and non-state actors in how they provide social services in different societies and/or turn to outsourcing and network governance.

3 Data and Methodology

This paper aims to identify, analyse and compare models of cooperation between local governments and NPOs in both Germany and China. The two country teams each chose two sample cities in their country.[8] In order to ensure comparability, the two teams selected cases of NPO–state cooperation in the four policy areas of education, employment, social assistance (including legal aid) and vulnerable groups, which are core areas of social services for migrants in both countries. In order to cross-check the results on the conditions that lead to the success or failure of cooperation, we also selected one case in each city that stakeholders considered a failure in this regard.[9] The two research teams went into the field to collect data from July 2018 to April 2019. In each city we selected five cases following an organisational approach and in accordance with the following criteria:

- All cases are cooperative efforts between an NPO and the local government
- All cases are programmes/projects that focus on services for migrants
- NPO size, age, migrant involvement in operations, funding source, competition, administrative level shall all vary.[10]

---

8 The sample cities were chosen to represent one of the largest cities in each country (Berlin, Guangzhou) and one medium-sized city (Cologne, Hangzhou) that function as economic hubs in their regions. All are immigrant cities with a well-established third sector. Berlin is the German capital and largest city in the country. As a city-state in the federal system, it enjoys relative freedom concerning policy development and implementation. Cologne, on the other hand, is subordinate to the state of North-Rhine Westphalia and bound to the guidelines and regulations dictated on the state level. Likewise, Guangzhou is relatively independent, and as one of the richest and largest cities in China, enjoys the status of "model city" for developing a public management system for migrants. Hangzhou is the capital and economic centre of Zhejiang province, but it develops and implements policy primarily in response to guidelines from provincial or national levels (Ketels 2019, 17). All four cities are strongly influenced by migration and turn to NPOs in seeking effective solutions to this challenge (Ketels 2019, 17–18, online available at: https://refubium.fu-berlin.de/handle/fub188/17676).

9 In our cases, failure means that the desired NPO–state cooperation did not take place, was aborted or did not achieve the desired outcomes. This does not necessarily mean that the NPO's project as such is a failure. Due to the difficulty of tracing cooperation that did not arise or no longer exists, the selection of failed cases turned out to be extremely difficult and in one city, Cologne, was ultimately unsuccessful.

10 See the appendix of this paper for an overview of the basic characteristics of the nineteen cases.

The German and Chinese research teams conducted interviews with managers and staff of the NPOs, their volunteers as well as with local government representatives. The authors of this paper were involved in all phases of the research. Backed by desktop research and observations, the interviews lay the foundation for the extensive case studies.

For this paper we applied a secondary analysis of the nineteen case study reports written by the two research teams based on their fieldwork. The aim was to identify characteristics and rationales of cooperation in the German and Chinese cases and find patterns for them across different societies. Working from existing research we tested earlier theories of state–NPO coop-eration by deduction and complemented these insights by inductively identifying the rationales underlying these cooperative relationships. We argue that while the characteristics are similar in Germany and China, the rationales behind the application of certain modes of cooperation are different.

In order to identify these characteristics, we used MAXQDA software to code the nineteen case-study reports according to the categories that we developed based on the theoretical framework of third-party government and network governance (see section 4). To identify the underlying rationales, we inductively developed the categories during the coding process. Transcriptions of the Chinese interviews and secondary literature were consulted when additional information was needed.

4 Outsourcing and Networking Theory

Since the early 1980s, third-sector research in Western countries has concentrated increasingly on the relationships between governments and NPOs. The realisation that modern welfare states rely on joint efforts by governments and third-sector organisations gave rise to various perspectives on this partnership focusing on NPO roles in policy processes, NPO activities, and the modes and/or effects of cooperation (Zimmer 2010). To analyse the state–NPO relationships in more depth, third-party government and network governance are concepts that successfully capture the complex relationships and operational work by the NPOs in both countries across all policy areas. By employing these two theories, we are able to examine the cooperative modes between NPOs and local governments from two sides: the third-party government concept offers a fruitful framework for analysing the top-down outsourcing mechanisms from government to NPOs, while the network governance approach sheds light on the bottom-up networking structures of NPOs that cooperate with govern-

ment. This section of the paper provides an overview of these two theoretical approaches.

4.1 Third-Party Government

In response to the fact that NPO–state cooperation was still a largely over-
looked topic, in the early 1980s Lester Salamon started to develop and explore the concept of "third-party government", which he summarised in
his book *Partners in Public Service: Government-Nonprofit Relations in the
Modern Welfare State* (Salamon 1995). He argues that a "lack of theory" was
responsible for neglecting the growth and significance of the third sector
in the United States. A new form of governance, which Salamon called
"third-party government", had developed and required a theory that acknowledges government–NPO partnerships and thereby goes beyond theories of the welfare state and the voluntary sector (ibid., 15–16). Under
"third-party government", NPOs fulfil various governmental functions.
Via different channels, the government transfers funds and responsibilities
to NPOs which become crucial actors in providing public services while at
the same time deriving large parts of their income from the government
(ibid., 33–34). The theory of the welfare state obscures this development
because it ascribes all authority for providing social services to the state
alone. Like-wise, theories of the voluntary sector such as "market failure/
government failure" cannot do justice to effective state–NPO partnerships
because they explain the existence of the non-profit sector solely as a substi-
tute for shortcomings of the government and the market. These theories
fail to explain regulated cooperation, government support for NPOs and
joint efforts for effective public management, and therefore it was necessary to redo the theory (ibid., 38–40). Salamon points out that the voluntary sector, like the government and the market, also has some inherent
limitations, such as limited resources, favouritism and/or a lack of professionalism (ibid., 44–45). As regards these kinds of voluntary sector and
government failure, it becomes apparent that both the non-profit sector
and the government can profit from a partner that can compensate for
their respective limitations. Salamon argues that "the voluntary sector's
weaknesses correspond well with government's strengths, and vice versa"
(ibid., 48). A collaborative partnership in which one actor does not replace
the other but in which government and NPOs join forces for effective public management would therefore be the most efficient solution. In other
words, the modern welfare state "[…] is an elaborate system of 'third-party
government' […], in which government shares a substantial degree of its

discretion over spending of public funds and the exercise of public authority with third-party implementers" (ibid., 41).

As a concept that accepts and formalises institutional pluralism, third-
party government is similar to contracting. However, it is more complex
and extends beyond contracting by not only including specified contracts
for service provision but possibly by entailing formalised tools such as
loans or insurance that transfer service provision to NPOs in more flexible
ways. Moreover, under third-party government the government not only
shares allocated funds with NPOs but also transfers the decision-making
authority on spending the funds and on public administration (Coston
1989, 369).

Our analysis in section 5 shows that the outsourcing of services from local governments to NPOs both in Germany and China is characterised by
many aspects of third-party government in different ways.

To identify the outsourcing characteristics by deductive means, we coded the case reports in our qualitative content analysis according to five basic criteria for state–NPO cooperation in Salamon's third-party government framework:

1. Existence of formalised cooperation: collaboration that is formalised in
   some way and in which the NPO is officially recognised
2. Transfer of administrative responsibilities: cooperation in which the
   NPO assumes public administration responsibilities
3. Complementary cooperative relationship: collaboration in which the
   functions and responsibilities of the state and NPO complement each
   other by balancing their respective strengths and limitations
4. Congruence of goals: cooperation which is based on congruent goals
   by the state and NPO regarding public administration
5. Favourable power relations: cooperation in which the state has a power
   advantage but the NPO also has a certain degree of autonomy and/or
   participation in decision-making.

4.2 Network Governance

Most of the case reports in our sample show a high degree of networking
on the part of the NPOs. Networks, or the embeddedness of (economic)
actors, were described most prominently by Granovetter in explaining economic exchanges (Granovetter 1992). Network governance theory originally derived from the observation that many industries were increasingly
using a form of coordination characterised by informal relationships rather

than by bureaucratic structures within organisations and formal contractual relationships in order to coordinate complex production procedures or services in uncertain and competitive environments. Network governance is a field of research that has recently received increased scholarly attention, particularly from the "top-down" perspective of governments networking with societal actors. Two examples of recently published and rather comprehensive works are Kapucu and Hu (2020) and Emerson and Nabatchi (2015). Kapucu and Hu offer a textbook on network governance, encompassing basic definitions, aspects of leadership, and also real-life applications of network governance. Emerson and Nabatchi published an equally comprehensive textbook on collaborative governance, illustrated by manifold case studies. These and other works on network governance and collaborative governance are approaches to analyse and understand the building of networks from the perspective of the government's governance – networks involving government actors/organs and societal actors.

The particular networks that we study in this article, however, are the "bottom-up" networks, the networks that are formed by NPOs facing the challenge of cooperating with the local governments. These networks are formed primarily among societal organisations but might also include government agents or organs. In other words, they are NPO networks within network governance/collaborative governance in the sense of government organs collaborating with societal actors.

For the purpose of analysing the particular needs and practices of this "bottom-up"-side of network governance, we find the article of Jones et al. (1997) particularly enlightening. In their explanation of when network-type relationships are likely to occur and how they can help the organisations involved (businesses or NPOs) resolve their problems, Candice Jones, William S. Hesterly and Stephen P. Borgatti (1997) integrated the concept of network governance and the theory of transaction cost economics. Basing their work on this approach, Jones et al. redefined network governance as follows:

> Network governance involves a select, persistent, and structured set of autonomous firms (as well as nonprofit agencies) engaged in creating products or services based on implicit and open-ended contracts to adapt to environmental contingencies and to coordinate and safeguard exchanges. These contracts are socially—not legally—binding. (Jones et al. 1997: 914)

By "select" they mean that network members usually form a subset of an industry in which they engage in frequent exchanges. "Persistent" denotes the dynamic process of organising and reorganising the network by its members. This definition describes the network exchanges as "structured" in the sense that they are "neither random nor uniform but rather are patterned, reflecting a division of labor". Finally, "implicit and open contracts" indicate that exchanges are not governed by authority structures or legal contracts, but are formed in a process of adapting and coordinating exchanges that relies on "social coordination and control, such as occupational socialisation, collective sanctions, and reputations". This does not exclude the existence of formal contracts among some members of the network as long as "these do not define the relations among all of the parties" (Jones et al. 1997, 914 ff.). In explaining why this form of governance is preferred by the organisations, Jones et al. use the basic ideas from transaction cost theory. They propose that organisations choose to engage in networks when environmental uncertainty demands adaption, the exchanges involve "unique equipment, processes, or knowledge developed by participants to complete exchanges, and the exchange is frequent, because frequent exchanges facilitate the transfer of tacit knowledge, facilitate embeddedness, and may provide cost efficiency" (Jones et al. 1997, 916).

Our analysis in section 5 shows that the cooperation betweeb NPOs and local governments both in Germany and China is characterised by different aspects of network governance.

To identify the existence and characteristics of network governance by deduction in the cooperative relationships between NPOs and local governments in our cases, we coded the case reports in our qualitative content analysis along the following four conditions proposed by Jones et al. as heuristic devices:

- Demand uncertainty: for this research project involving non-profit actors, we slightly adapted the original uncertainty of (market) *demand* to an uncertainty of *funding*
- Asset specificity, i.e. particular knowledge, skills or other assets are necessary to provide the required services
- Task complexity, i.e. the service to be provided involves a number of parties and subtasks that need special coordination
- High exchange frequency, i.e. regular exchange in the networks over a lengthy span of time [11].

In the next section we analyse the research reports.

---

11 The analytical part will concentrate on the first three heuristic devices. As for the high exchange frequency, we assume it is given in all the networks we analyse, otherwise we would not consider the network to exist (see 5.2.1).

5 Analysis: State–NPO Cooperation in Migrant Service Provision in China and Germany

This analysis comprises two parts: First, we analyse whether and how social services are outsourced in the two countries. Using the criteria of Salamon's third-party government theory, we show that and how outsourcing takes place. We also identify the rationales behind outsourcing from the perspective of the local governments. Second, we identify and examine the rationales behind networking behaviour by the NPOs, using the network governance theory as proposed by Jones et al. as an analytical device.[12]

5.1 Outsourcing Trends in Comparison

The cooperation between local governments and NPOs in social service provision is defined by the the outsourcing of activities from the former to the latter in most of the German and Chinese case studies. This section explores the characteristics of and rationales behind these outsourcing activities. Salamon's third-party government concept (1995) is used as a tool to deduce the characteristics of the outsourcing systems by analysing the case studies according to the five criteria of third-party government as explained in section 4. We will then explicate the rationales underlying the outsourcing activities, which were identified in the inductive content analysis.

5.1.1 Outsourcing Characteristics

Outsourcing activities from local governments to NPOs can be observed in fifteen of the nineteen cases analysed in this paper. Of these fifteen outsourcing cases seven cases fulfil all five third-party government criteria in one way or another and eight cases fulfil three or four of the criteria. The four cases that display no outsourcing activities also hardly meet the third-party government criteria. They are the three cases of unsuccessful cooperation and one German grassroots organisation that does not maintain any

---

12 The analysis largely refers to the nineteen case study reports that have been analysed with the help of MAXQDA. References to the reports are derived from MAXQDA and are displayed in footnotes as follows: City\Policy Field_NPO Name: Paragraph.

direct cooperation with the local government (Berliner Stadtmission/Refugio (Refugio)). The German case of Kein Abseits! e.V. (Kein Abseits) and the Chinese case of Guangzhou Dinghe Social Work Service Center (Dinghe), which show third-party government characteristics in an archetypal way, will be used below to illustrate the analysis criteria.

Kein Abseits is a Berlin-based association that offers mentoring services for child and youth refugees to enhance their opportunities. This NPO started in 2011 as a small private initiative and gradually grew as both the demand for services and its willingness to engage increased. In 2016 it began working with the government under the auspices of the Master Plan for Integration and Security (*Masterplan Sicherheit und Integration*—hereafter "Master Plan") developed to address the administrative challenges arising from the large numbers of refugees entering the country after 2015.

Dinghe is a non-profit service centre for homeless people in Guangzhou. It developed out of volunteer work and was able to register as a private non-enterprise unit (民办非企业单位, PNUs)[13] in 2013 with the help of a private sponsor and the support of the local civil affairs bureau. In 2014 it won a contract in a competitive bidding process to receive government funding for a social assistance project for homeless people, and thereby began developing a closer collaborative relationship with the local authorities.

Both NPOs fulfil government functions and cooperate with local authorities in accordance with the third-party government criteria. However, Kein Abseits appears to pursue its own agenda within this framework, while Dinghe is developing into an agent of the state.

The next sections analyse and compare the outsourcing cases according to the five third-party government criteria. Each section uses the two example cases to illustrate archetypal fulfilment of the criteria.

1. Existence of Formalised Cooperation

According to the third-party government concept, an NPO has to be officially recognised and cooperation must be formalised in some way to be successful. Contracting is a common form of formalised cooperation, but

---

13 Private non-enterprise units (PNUs) (民办非企业单位) are one of three officially regulated types of NPOs in Chinese law; the other two are foundations (基金会) and membership-based associations (社会团体). Since the introduction of the Charity Law in 2016, PNUs have been renamed social service organisations (社会服务机构).

the third-party government concept goes beyond this to include other co-operative structures as well.

In all cases of successful cooperation in our sample, the NPOs are officially registered, a condition which grants them state recognition and the ability to act as legal entities on their own. The German NPOs in our sample are registered either as associations (e.V.) or private limited liability companies with public benefit status (gGmbH). The Chinese NPOs are registered as PNUs or membership-based associations (社会团体).

Kein Abseits! e.V. (Kein Abseits) is a registered non-profit association. In 2016 it answered a call for tenders from the Senate Department for Education, Youth and Family and entered a contractual relationship to receive funding for providing services in connection with the Master Plan.[14] It has since also become officially recognised as a provider of child and youth welfare services (*Träger der freien Kinder- und Jugendhilfe*).[15] It and similar NPOs receive funds from the German state on a contract basis for innovative and efficient solutions to challenges in service provision to refugees (see also e.g. RheinFlanke gGmbH (Rheinflanke), Auszugsmanagement, AWO Kreisverband Südost (AWO)).

In China, straightforward contracting usually takes place within a framework promoted in recent years, by which the government purchases services (e.g. Superior Power Social Work Development Center (Superior Power), GZ Lawyers Association, Dinghe, Zhejiang Xiezhi vocational college (Xiezhi), Qidian Yixing). In Dinghe's case the local government in Guangzhou started a service-purchasing initiative because it alone could no longer handle the increasing numbers of homeless people, mostly migrant workers.[16] Because Dinghe's service provision met the requirements of the government, the Guangzhou civil affairs bureau and the NPO signed their first three-year contract in 2015. Since then, the Dinghe NPO provides the services in the contract and the government not only funds the daily expenses but has also purchased five additional projects.[17]

These examples show contracting to be the most common form of formalised cooperation in our German–Chinese sample. All fifteen outsourcing cases meet the criteria of formal cooperation in one way or another. In other forms of formalised cooperation the government employs or directly finances the project coordinator (e.g. Bridge network (Bridge), Chance+

---

14 Berlin\Education_Kein Abseits_Berlin: 54 – 54.
15 Berlin\Education_Kein Abseits_Berlin: 15 – 15.
16 Guangzhou_en\Vulnerable Groups_Dinghe Social Workers: 3 – 3.
17 Guangzhou_en\Vulnerable Groups_Dinghe Social Workers: 24 – 24.

Netzwerk Flüchtlinge, and Arbeit (Chance+), Agisra),[18] or the cooperation developed out of a joint idea and is based on an agreement that regulates the responsibilities of the parties involved (Guangdong Beida Economic and Trade College (Beida College)).[19] In China, formalised cooperation can also display characteristics of a top-down government project when the government establishes and completely controls the NPO's work based on a cooperation contract (HZ Lawyers Association, GZ Lawyers Association).[20]

2. Transfer of Administrative Responsibilities

The involvement of NPOs in public administration processes and the transfer of responsibilities from the government to NPOs is another criterion of third-party government, which specifies the form of cooperation between the state and an NPO.

Apart from the formalised cooperation described above, Kein Abseits is also involved in various public administration structures and not only receives government funding but also exercises public authority and assumes certain responsibilities. In its part of the city, the organisation is acknowledged as an important actor and influences public decision-making.[21] As co-founder of the "Netzwerk Kinderpatenschaften"—a network of Berlin social organisations that offer mentoring services—Kein Abseits has an impact on Berlin's social agenda and organises the distribution of mentoring services for refugees throughout the whole city.[22]

Dinghe provides policy supervision and service guidance, and assumes government functions so as to increase awareness and satisfy the basic needs of the people in Guangzhou.[23] For example, it submitted a policy proposal in 2017 on NPO social services for the homeless,[24] and regularly publishes handbooks on NPO areas of work which not only provide guid-

---

18 Berlin\Employment_Bridge: 86 – 86; Cologne\Employment_Chance+: 8 – 8.

19 Guangzhou_en\Education_Beida College: 44 – 44.

20 Guangzhou_en\Social Assistance_GZ Lawyers Association: 49 – 49; Hangzhou_en\Social Assistance_HZ Lawyers Association: 30 – 30.

21 Berlin\Education_Kein Abseits_Berlin: 7 – 7.

22 Berlin\Education_Kein Abseits_Berlin: 45 – 45.

23 Guangzhou_en\Vulnerable Groups_Dinghe Social Workers: 58 – 58.

24 The paper is called "Policy Proposal to Actively Guide the Intervention of Social Forces in Providing Social Assistance to Vagrants and Beggars".

ance to social workers and NPOs but also seek to have an impact on public administration.[25]

This type of transfer of administrative responsibilities from governments to NPOs can be observed in seven of the cases in our sample. They fulfil all third-party government criteria of being intensely involved in governance processes and are exemplary cases of outsourcing.

3. Complementary Cooperative Relationship

Salamon (1995, 48) argues that both the state and NPOs have inherent limitations and that they therefore need cooperation partners. In the third-party government concept, the strengths of NPOs counterbalance the limitations of the state and vice versa. Cooperation is therefore characterised by a complementary distribution of functions and responsibilities.

Cooperation between Kein Abseits and the local government developed to address an urgent need on both sides. The NPO was facing financial and sustainability difficulties and struggling to gain public trust because many people hesitated to trust an organisation that was not well known and did not have the support of the government.[26] At the same time, the local government was facing huge challenges in providing services to the incoming refugees and its administrative structures could not deal adequately with social inequalities.[27] The biggest strength of Kein Abseits was its large number of volunteers and its innovative and flexible portfolio which the local authorities could not offer.[28] For its part, the local government was able to provide funds, development prospects and greater public recognition for the organisation.

Dinghe's cooperation with the government developed out of similar needs. The local government lacked the expertise and human resources to provide services for homeless people in Guangzhou and therefore sought a partner who could provide them.[29] Dinghe was the first NPO to provide such services in Guangzhou and was ready to fill this gap.[30] At the same time, it depends on regular funding and administrative support and there-

---

25 Guangzhou_en\Vulnerable Groups_Dinghe Social Workers: 50 – 50,
     Guangzhou_en\Vulnerable Groups_Dinghe Social Workers: 50 – 50.
26 Berlin\Education_Kein Abseits_Berlin: 40 – 40.
27 Berlin\Education_Kein Abseits_Berlin: 33 – 33.
28 Berlin\Education_Kein Abseits_Berlin: 68 – 68.
29 Guangzhou_en\Vulnerable Groups_Dinghe Social Workers: 9 – 9.
30 Guangzhou_en\Vulnerable Groups_Dinghe Social Workers: 9 – 9.

fore depends on the complementary function of the government as the purchaser of the services.[31]

A complementary cooperative relationship between the state and NPOs appears to be a basic precondition for a functioning outsourcing relationship; certainly, all the outsourcing cases in our sample fulfil this criterion. A key function of the NPOs is the provision of services the government does not provide but considers important. This is a distinct tendency in the Chinese cases, where many services are not covered by social policy. For example, Xiezhi built a much-needed education and employment system in Hangzhou and won government support because the local administration failed to bear this responsibility and welcomed the opportunity to outsource the task.[32] In Germany, NPOs more commonly serve a bridging function between the government and the target group. They help the government gain better access to the target group (e.g. Bridge, AWO), support refugees in dealing with the complicated bureaucratic structures (e.g. Rheinflanke), and communicate directly with the target groups—all tasks which the local authorities apparently cannot accomplish (e.g. Chance+). Another important function of NPOs is to introduce expertise and innovative solutions, which often means that they train both public and private actors (e.g. Chance+, Xiezhi, Superior Power).

Besides allocating resources, the state also fulfils the function of providing a support environment for the NPOs. This is particularly important in China, where NPOs depend on a favourable political environment in order to operate and gain some influence. The case of the Xiezhi NPO illustrates this function particularly well in its efforts to develop a cooperative relationship with the local government in order to receive policy support and create a good environment for its own development, even though it has sufficient private assets and does not depend on government resources.[33]

4. Congruence of Goals

A basic precondition for successful cooperation according to the third-party government concept is the pursuit of congruent public administration goals by the state and NPOs.

---

31 Guangzhou_en\Vulnerable Groups_Dinghe Social Workers: 27 – 27.
32 Hangzhou_en\Employment Xiezhi: 30 – 30.
33 Hangzhou_en\Employment Xiezhi: 29 – 29.

Kein Abseits has an intrinsic motivation to improve the situation of young refugees. This NPO's vision is to create a society where everybody is engaged in volunteer work and where the social inclusion of refugees is a matter of course which does not need the support of public authorities anymore.[34] With the development of the Berlin government's Master Plan, which lists societal participation by refugees and civic engagement as key objectives, these goals officially became part of the public agenda.[35]

Dinghe assumes responsibility for social services that are desired by the government. In 2012, the Chinese central government issued the Guiding Opinions of the Ministry of Civil Affairs on Promoting Social Forces to Participate in Social Assistance to Vagrants and Beggars, which make this cooperation an important goal for the local government.[36] As an organisation operating in lieu of the state, the NPO adapts to the goals of the local administration in this case.[37]

Cooperation in our sample is based mainly on common public administration goals. In both countries, state–NPO cooperation is only successful if the basic goals of the NPO correspond with the political agenda of the state. However, in Germany it is possible and common practice for NPOs to criticise existing public structures and advocate the different implementation of political goals (e.g. Bridge, Agisra),[38] while the Chinese organisations see their role more as advisors to than advocates for the government (e.g. Superior Power, Dinghe).[39]

5. Favourable Power Relations

According to the third-party government concept, a favourable power relation is one in which the state has the advantage yet the NPOs cannot be completely overruled and must also have some influence.

Cooperation between Kein Abseits and the local administration is based on the guidelines stated in the policy agendas for providing social services to refugees, i.e. on the Master Plan and its follow-up, the Overall Concept for the Integration and Participation of Refugees (*Gesamtkonzept zur Inte-*

---

34 Berlin\Education_Kein Abseits_Berlin: 32 – 32.

35 Berlin\Education_Kein Abseits_Berlin: 53 – 53.

36 Guangzhou_en\Vulnerable Groups_Dinghe Social Workers: 60 – 60.

37 Guangzhou_en\Vulnerable Groups_Dinghe Social Workers: 50 – 50.

38 Berlin\Employment_Bridge: 97 – 97.

39 Guangzhou_en\Employment_Superior Power: 9 – 9; Guangzhou_en\Employment_Superior Power: 9 – 9.

gration und Teilhabe Geflüchteter). Kein Abseits first had to apply for funds and adapt to the requirements of these government concepts. While this led to a structural imbalance of power in favour of the state, the NPO could still influence the policymaking process. It managed to become a relevant and established player in local public administration and was therefore able to build a cooperative relationship with local authorities based on mutual trust and understanding. On this basis, the NPO gradually enjoyed greater autonomy and authority.[40]

Dinghe signed a contract with the local government that determines the rights and obligations of both parties. It specifies instructions for the execution of service provision by the NPO and grants the government the right to supervise and assess project implementation. If the government is not satisfied with the NPO's performance, it can terminate the contract and refuse to pay any further funds.[41] The government therefore has a strong power advantage in this cooperative relationship, and the NPO must conform to the government's requirements if it wants to sustain the relationship. However, Dinghe is successful in offering services that the government cannot provide, and the local authorities therefore depend on its capabilities. The NPO successfully influences policymaking and has an independent board of directors, which manages its daily business.[42]

The legal basis can therefore grant more power to the government in such a form of cooperation, but successful and self-confident NPOs can develop their own influence and keep a certain level of autonomy. Besides guidelines, regulations and contracts designed by the state, the government's power usually derives from resources that it can terminate any time or from approval that it must renew at regular intervals (e.g. Bridge, AWO, Beida College, Qidian Yixing). Staff overlaps, when for example the NPO project coordinator is employed by a public agency, also function as an instrument of control (Bridge, Chance+).[43] In the Chinese case of cooperative relations, the government generally clearly holds a dominant position. Only by winning the trust of the government and pursuing goals that it favours can the NPOs work relatively undisturbed, assume public responsibilities and even influence decision-making processes (e.g. Superior Power).[44] Twelve of the fifteen outsourcing cases in our sample fulfil this crite-

---

40 Berlin\Education_Kein Abseits_Berlin: 69 – 69.
41 Guangzhou_en\Vulnerable Groups_Dinghe Social Workers: 27 – 27.
42 Guangzhou_en\Vulnerable Groups_Dinghe Social Workers: 61 – 61;
    Guangzhou_en\Vulnerable Groups_Dinghe Social Workers: 8 – 8.
43 Berlin\Employment_Bridge: 65 – 65.
44 Guangzhou_en\Employment_Superior Power: 54 – 54.

rion. The exception in Germany does not stand in a hierarchical relationship with the government (Agisra), while the Chinese exceptions are completely controlled by the government and have no autonomy at all (Hangzhou and GZ Lawyers Association).

5.1.2 Rationales Behind Outsourcing Services by Local Governments

The analysis of outsourcing characteristics shows that services are outsourced from local governments to NPOs in fifteen of the nineteen case studies. Four main government motivations for doing so are identified: 1) to support the provision of public services; 2) to fulfil guidelines set by higher administrative levels; 3) to derive support from NPO expertise; and 4) in the Chinese cases: to maintain control and social stability. These four categories are examined below to determine the rationales behind local government outsourcing of services to NPOs.

1. Support Public Service Provision

In all outsourcing cases, cooperation with the NPO was established to support the government in providing public services. Its character depends on whether the state offers any services in the respective policy area itself and whether the NPO offers the same services or complements those of the government. Competing parallel services by the state and an NPO in the same field occur only in cases that do not have the characteristics of outsourcing from the local government to the NPO. Outsourcing therefore happens when NPOs complement government services to improve efficiency and effectiveness of service provision or when they provide services the state would otherwise not offer, also to improve efficacy (see Table 1).

Table 1: Characteristics of NPO support for public services provision

	The state offers social services in this field	The state does not offer social services in this field
The NPO offers the same services in parallel to the state	Competing services (no outsourcing)	X
The NPO services complement the state services	Improve efficiency and effectiveness of service provision (German outsourcing model)	X
The NPO offers services the state does not	X	Facilitate efficacy of services (Chinese outsourcing model)

In all the German outsourcing cases, the NPOs complement the services provided by the local government. This implies that the local administrations in Germany offer services in all the policy areas that we studied, but these are not sufficient or require support and NPOs to fill gaps. Except for the two networks, Bridge and Chance+, which were founded as part of the federal programme European Social Fund Integration Guideline (*ESF, Integrationsrichtlinie Bund*) to build local networks, in all German cases the NPOs initiated their projects and took action to foster cooperation with the local government. They develop projects where there are problems and gaps in service provision by the state, and local administrations develop cooperation with these NPOs to support and direct their work and to make use of their expertise and innovative capacities. In these cases, cooperative relations serve to improve the efficiency and effectiveness of services. On the one hand, NPOs offer efficient solutions in contrast to what can be the bureaucratic and inflexible characteristics of local administrations in Germany. For example, the Kein Abseits NPO offers low threshold mentoring and education services for refugees who cannot benefit from services offered by the city's administration because the bureaucratic preconditions and hurdles are insurmountable.[45] In the case of Auszugsmanagement in Cologne, the NPOs in the network have developed a system to provide cheap and flexible housing options for refugees and approached the city's administration to work together with them for better housing conditions. Because ongoing demand had pushed municipal services to their limits, the city took Auszugsmanagement's more efficient solution into its service portfolio.[46] On the other hand, NPOs support the effectiveness of government services when e.g. the local administration struggles to access the target group. The NPOs build bridges between the target group and the administration and thereby support the latter's services. Especially when NPOs deal with vulnerable groups, good connections and a basis of trust are needed. For example, AWO in Berlin and Agisra in Cologne both have a long tradition of offering social services for women in need and facilitating female refugees' access to public services.[47]

The Chinese cases of successful cooperation show a different picture of the nature of NPO support for public services. While the German outsourcing models in our cases complement the government services, the

---

45 Berlin\Education_Kein Abseits_Berlin: 33 – 33.
46 Cologne\Social Assistance_Auszugsmanagement: 58 – 58.
47 Berlin\Vulnerable Groups_AWO Frauenberatung: 46 – 46; Cologne\Vulnerable groups_Agisra: 44 – 44.

NPOs in the Chinese cases offer services the state would otherwise not provide (see Table 1). This implies that the Chinese state cannot or does not want to provide its own services in the policy areas studied but instead relies on third-party providers to do so. The cases in our sample fall into three different categories: 1) the government takes the lead and initiates the project and cooperation (Superior Power, GZ and HZ Lawyers Associations, Dinghe, Qidian Yixing Social Work Development Center (Qidian Yixing)); 2) the NPOs are the initiators and the government then transfers the responsibility for these services to the NPO (Hangzhou Net, Xiezhi); and 3) one case in which the government and NPO take joint action to tackle a social problem (Beida College). In all these cases, the NPOs make public service provision more effective. In the Chinese cases, the state wants to take pressure off local administrations and develop solutions to social challenges at the same time. With the lawyers' associations in Guangzhou and Hangzhou, for example, this happens in a top-down manner, by which the government establishes the NPOs and directs their actions to create public services. By contrast, Xiezhi in Hangzhou is a bottom-up development, by which services are provided that were originally the responsibility of the government, but the local administration did not succeed and subsequently embraced the solution offered by the NPO.[48] In other cases, social services provided by NPOs are arranged by the government to deal with new challenges resulting from large numbers of migrant workers entering the cities. One example would be Superior Power in Guangzhou, where the local government has responded to social unrest and asked the NPO to develop new services.[49]

2. Fulfil Guidelines Set by Higher Administrative Levels

In both Germany and China, local governments have additional reasons for establishing cooperative relationships with NPOs, such as the need to follow guidelines from higher administrative levels. In nine of the fifteen outsourcing cases in our sample, concrete guidelines or programs are mentioned as a reason for the local government to seek cooperation with NPOs. The respective guidelines are city-specific. In Berlin, the Master Plan has strongly promoted state–society cooperation to integrate refugees. In Cologne, no such overall programme for refugees has been instituted

---

48 Hangzhou_en\Employment_Xiezhi: 30 – 30.
49 Guangzhou_en\Employment_Superior Power: 52 – 52.

but smaller guidelines, such as the city council's decision to promote the integration of refugee children and youth, have influenced cooperation in our case studies.

In China, Guangzhou has the special status of "Model City for Service and Management of Floating Population and Ethnic Minorities", which means that the central government regards it as a pioneer city with pilot state–society cooperative projects to integrate the floating population (Ketels 2019, 7). All successful cases in Guangzhou have developed as a result of this status and the corresponding expectations. Several additional guidelines such as the Guangzhou Social Work Service Matrix of "General Service + Specialized Service" or the "Guiding Opinions of the Ministry of Civil Affairs on Promoting Social Forces to Participate in the Social Assistance to Vagrants and Beggars", have further promoted cooperation in our sample. In Hangzhou, the influence of such guidelines is much weaker. Except for the lawyers' association, which was founded in accordance with national guidelines, no superior guidelines are mentioned. The majority of cases in Hangzhou are projects that developed out of grassroots movements or individual engagement and were later engaged by the government (Hangzhou Net Volunteer Branch (HZ Net), Xiezhi, Home of Grassroots (Grassroots)).

3. Derive Support from NPO Expertise

Another objective of local governments in cooperating with NPOs is to benefit from NPO expertise in their policymaking processes and/or make use of NPO abilities to train public officials and social workers. Eight case studies explicitly give this rationale, with no difference in meaning between China and Germany. For Bridge and Chance+ in Germany, for example, the ESF Integration Guideline, which promotes and funds the cooperation explicitly states the goal of gaining experience and providing information to policymakers and other public actors. In China, projects and cooperation with e.g. the lawyers' associations in Hangzhou and Guangzhou are explicitly developed by the government to utilise the expertise of the lawyers for government objectives.

4. Maintain Control and Social Stability

The fourth rationale has only been identified in the Chinese cases. Maintaining control and social stability is a factor mentioned in every Chinese case as a major reason for local governments to cooperate with NPOs in providing social services. This factor has two aspects: on the one hand, the government wants to reduce risks to social stability by addressing factors in social unrest and entrusts the NPOs with doing so. In the case of Dinghe, for example, the government is seeking a way to deal with the potential for social unrest arising from homeless people on the streets of Guangzhou and consequently initiates cooperation with an NPO that offers solutions. On the other hand, the government seeks to control and channel the productivity of certain groups in accordance with government objectives. As regards the lawyers' associations, for example, the NPOs serve to control and utilise legal specialists by issuing lists of lawyers' social responsibilities and recruiting them for voluntary services directed by government agencies.[50] In the case of Beida College the NPO helps to channel and control the migrant workforce as desired by local government to avoid social unrest and promote Guangzhou's development.[51]

5.2 Networking Trends in Comparison

All the cases in our sample applied networking to various degrees in their work strategies. In this section we first—inductively—describe the various networking activities[52] that occurred in our case studies (5.2.1); in a second step we then apply—deductively—the operationalised theory of Jones et al. (1997) on network governance to understand the rationales behind these networking activities (5.2.2). Since networking is an essential part of

---

50 Guangzhou_en\Social Assistance_GZ Lawyers Association: 37 – 37.
51 Guangzhou_en\Education_Beida College: 68 – 68.
52 In practice, the boundaries between cooperation and networking can be blurred. For the analysis in this report, we distinguish cooperation and networking as follows: Cooperation is directly related to the creation of the product/service that is offered by the NPO, whereas networking activities indirectly support this creative process. For example, cooperation is the case when the local government signs a contract with or informally has the NPO provide a certain service, whereas networking applies when the NPO and representatives of local state authorities meet regularly at roundtable meetings to ensure similar understanding of the services the state purchases from the NPO.

the work of all the organisations in our sample, this section will not feature a "model case" but rather analyse and compare the cases according to the categories developed from the literature on network governance.

5.2.1 Existence of Networks

As mentioned above, all the NPOs in our cases were embedded in some kind of network, albeit to different degrees and of different network size. We identified the following types: 1) those centring around German and Chinese organisations that are themselves organised as networks; 2) German and Chinese organisations that have built complex stakeholder networks; 3) German networks that explicitly do not include government agents; and 4) Chinese networks that are under the supervision and leadership of a local government agent.

First, some of the NPOs are themselves networks: in Germany Chance+ and Bridge are networks comprising other NPOs, government agents, other networks and cooperation partners for service provision. In both cases, the government had explicitly looked for networked organisations in the bidding process.[53] In the case of Auszugsmanagement, the local government itself has started organising coordination meetings to build up the network in order to find accommodation for refugees.[54] In the case of the AWO Kreisverband, it is embedded in the large network of the umbrella organisation AWO. Beida College can also be placed in this category, as a network of the Guangdong Beida College of Economics and Trade, the Beida Alumni Association, other universities and the Guangdong Provincial Government.[55] Kein Abseits is similarly a network and has initiated several new networks as well. That includes contacts with sponsors and with many other organisations and institutions to recruit mentors for their programmes. This network is composed primarily of stakeholders and involves only few government agents.

Second, other organisations are not set up as networks themselves but have built up networks that include all relevant stakeholders of the respective project(s) they conduct and the services they offer. Xiezhi in Hangzhou, for instance, has built a network that connects the organisation with various levels of government agencies and Communist Party officials

---

53 Cologne\Employment_Chance+: 60 - 60, Berlin\Employment_Bridge: 50 – 50.
54 Cologne\Social Assistance_Auszugsmanagement: 14 – 14.
55 Guangzhou_en\Education_Beida College: 3 – 3.

in Hangzhou City, Zhejiang Province and the capital Beijing. A considerable portion of the network consists of funders: Xiezhi is funded by various foundations (YouChange Entrepreneur Foundation for Poverty Alleviation, Zengai Charity Foundation, and Zhejiang Women and Children Foundation) and by large enterprises such as Alibaba. The network also includes companies that are potential employers for the migrant workers lodged at and trained by Xiezhi's different facilities and the universities that use its big data employment intermediation services. In addition, the leader of Xiezhi is a member of the board of a regional development centre (which might also be interested in the services Xiezhi offers). Xiezhi also maintains close relations with all important media agencies and outlets. Similarly, the German organisation Refugio is centred around a shared housing space and coffee shop, and has built a network that consists of all the important stakeholders. It is managed by the Berliner Stadtmission, which is under the umbrella of the Protestant Church, which is a huge network organisation itself. Like Xiezhi, Refugio also combines its social services with for-profit enterprises, albeit on a smaller scale. The Refugio café is an enterprise that helps finance the organisation's work, but it is also the venue for language courses for Refugio's target group and simultaneously a channel through which the organisation involves its neighbourhood in its endeavours. Furthermore, it maintains a relationship with the Technical University in Berlin by helping to design a rooftop garden for the university. Rheinflanke is organised around its services for young people in homes for asylum seekers, and offers leisure activities and education programmes. It is organised in the form of a stakeholder network that includes sponsors, resources for its services and government agents, i.e. complementary providers of services, skilled personnel and expertise. These stakeholder networks generally include government agents.

Third, another group (in Germany only) is embedded in networks that do not include government officials. Agisra is such a case. It is a member of the umbrella organisation Deutscher Paritätischer Wohlfahrtsverband, as well as of other working groups and networks (German and international). It has initiated an umbrella association itself and cooperates with the media. Agisra does not receive funds from the government. Be an Angel, one of the cases that turned out to be unsuccessful in terms of its cooperation with the local government, is another example of an NPO with a network that tends to exclude government-related members.

Fourth, in several Chinese cases, the government agents have supervisory functions in the networks of which they are members. For instance, Dinghe's project for homeless people in Guangzhou is part of the local government's network of "rescue stations" on municipal and district levels and a volunteer service that is also supervised by the local government's office of social affairs. Although the two lawyers' associations in Hangzhou and Guangzhou are huge networks,[56] due to their politically sensitive membership (lawyers and law firms) and the work they do (counselling in labour disputes), they are closely supervised by the local governments of their localities. Superior Power also belongs to this category of networks, having been invited by the government to take over research and supervision work for the government. Like other Chinese organisations, it has instituted a certain network in its governance structure, with three external directors on its board, one each from the media, a university and a law firm. HZ Net is a branch organisation of the Hangzhou Charity Federation, which is a membership-based non-governmental organisation in the city. It has an extensive network due to the widespread connections of the Hangzhou Charity Federation, consisting of media and government representatives and volunteer recruitment resources. According to the field report, the local government has a guiding role that extends beyond the service contract signed between it and HZ Net.

The three cases in our sample which we regard as having failed in their cooperation with the government are embedded in networks as follows. The Volunteer Service for Sanitation Workers (Sanitation Workers) has a very small network that consists primarily of its volunteers on the one hand and of the sanitation station and community neighbourhood committee on the other, which have to be considered representatives of the local state in the organisation's area of activity. One reason for the inability to extend the network seems to be the fact that Sanitation Workers was not able to register officially and therefore cannot act as a legal entity on its own. The second Chinese "failed" case is Grassroots. This organisation initially had a network of sponsors but subsequently lost all its connections to them when it became part of the local government administration. The fact that its legal status was unclear, because it was not registered as a social organisation but as a business enterprise, may have contributed to its problems. The German "failed" case, Be an Angel, is embedded in a network of type 3 (a stakeholder network without particularly close government relations). The field report explains its failure in part by the weak relationships among the network's members.

---

56 According to the field reports, the Guangzhou Lawyers Network has 15,000 individual and 700 group members, while the Hangzhou Lawyers Network has 7,213 individual members and 487 group members.

Table 2 provides an overview of the types of networks we identified in our sample cases.

Table 2: Overview of network types of sample cases

NPO name	Network type
Kein Abseits! e.V.	(1) Network organisation
Bridge Network	(1) Network organisation
AWO Kreisverband Südost Women's Counselling Center	(1) Network organisation
Chance+ Netzwerk Flüchtlinge und Arbeit	(1) Network organisation
Auszugsmanagement	(1) Network organisation
广东北达经贸专修学院 Guangdong Beida Economic and Trade College	(1) Network organisation
Berliner Stadtmission (Refugio)	(2) Stakeholder network
RheinFlanke gGmbH	(2) Stakeholder network
杭州市慈善总会杭州网义工分会 Hangzhou Net Volunteer Branch of Hangzhou Charity Federation	(2) Stakeholder network
浙江携职专修学院 Zhejiang Xiezhi Vocational College	(2) Stakeholder network
Be an Angel e.V.	(3) Network exclusive of government agents
AGISRA e.V.	(3) Network exclusive of government agents
广州市黄埔区优势力社会工作发展中心 Superior Power Social Work Development Center	(4) Stakeholder network, supervised by local government
广州市律师协会 Guangzhou Lawyers Association	(4) Stakeholder network, supervised by local government
广州市鼎和社会工作服务中心 Guangzhou Dinghe Social Work Service Center	(4) Stakeholder network, supervised by local government
杭州律师协会 Hangzhou Lawyers Association	(4) Stakeholder network, supervised by local government
杭州市下城区起点益行社会工作发展中心 Qidian Yixing Social Work Development Center	(4) Stakeholder network, supervised by local government
关爱环卫工人志愿服务队 Volunteer Service for Sanitation Workers	Apparently, very small or no functioning network.[57]
草根之家 Home of the Grassroots	Apparently, no functioning network.[58]

Table 2 shows first of all that all the organisations in our sample work in networks, and second that different variants seem to be more common in one country than in the other. Most of the German cases are network organisations themselves embedded in larger stakeholder networks. Organisations embedded in stakeholder networks with and without government agents exist in both Germany and China. While, in Germany we see stakeholder networks with and without government agents, the dominant Chi-

---

57 The Volunteer Service for Sanitation workers uses its network, which is mainly composed of the neighbourhood committee members, mainly for recruiting volunteer workers.

58 The network of this organisation, which was mainly composed of sponsors, dissolved completely after the organisation took up relations with the government.

nese variant in our sample is an organisation embedded in a stakeholder network under the supervision of the local government.

5.2.2 Rationales behind NPO Networking

We will now look at the rationales behind the networking activities of the NPOs in our sample. According to Jones et al. (1997), organisations tend to make use of network governance under three exchange conditions: 1. asset specificity, i.e. when the NPOs need special skills and knowledge to offer their services; 2. funding uncertainty, i.e. when the NPOs work under conditions such as short-term funding or fierce competition in government bidding processes that make long-term planning difficult; 3. task complexity, i.e. when the organisations conduct tasks that involve multiple stakeholders and/or multiple problems and/or require multiple kinds of expertise.

1. Exchange Condition: Asset Specificity

Jones et al. found evidence that business organisations tend to build networks when they need special knowledge and skills to deliver their products. We find that this also pertains to the NPOs in our case studies. The field reports analysed contain ample evidence of the NPOs maintaining networks in order to utilise the skills and knowledge of their different members. In particular, the NPOs use these assets to: (1) improve their visibility in the public sphere and the media; (2) ensure access to vital information for their work; (3) make use of for-profit entities for their non-profit work; (4) ensure access to expert knowledge for the provision of their services; and (5) function as an information platform in their field of expertise as one of the services in their portfolios.

(1) Improving NPO Visibility

Despite the different roles of the media and the different degrees of media freedom in Germany and China, we found that the NPOs in our sample maintain close relations to news media representatives in both countries. Beida College worked together with the Southern Newspaper Group, Guangdong Telecom Company and Xinhua Net in raising funds and doing promotional activities during the start-up phase of its organisation.[59] Superior Power invited a reporter from the Yangcheng Evening News onto its board of directors.[60] The founders of Xiezhi and of Dinghe are trained media professionals themselves (news anchorman and journalist). The interviewees from HZ Net also underscored the organisation's media connections.[61] The restaurant managed by Be an Angel is praised in the media,[62] and Be an Angel also uses the media for advocacy purposes.[63] Rheinflanke's board of trustees is "manned with celebrities from film and television [...]".[64]

(2) Ensuring NPO Access to Information Vital for their Work

Successful NPOs need access to government information, including administrative requirements and bidding processes. Many of them therefore include government personnel in their networks (as shown in section 5.2.1 on network existence). While government connections are usually the best choice for Chinese NPOs in terms of informational access, in Germany connections to one of the big umbrella organisations or churches can also be helpful in this respect. Accordingly, many of our sample NPOs are in fact members of umbrella organisations: Agisra and Rheinflanke are members of the Deutscher Paritätischer Wohlfahrtsverband, [65] Chance+ Network and Auszugsmanagement belong to the Catholic Caritas Verband,[66] and the AWO Kreisverband is part of the Arbeiterwohlfahrt (AWO).

(3) Making Use of For-Profit Entities for their Non-profit Work

A number of NPOs in our sample combined their welfare services with business enterprises, often coffee shops or restaurants but also other for-

---

59 Guangzhou_en\Education_Beida College: 48 – 48.
60 Guangzhou_en\Employment_Superior Power: 12 – 12.
61 Hangzhou_en\Education_HZ Net Voluntary Branch: 31– 31.
62 Berlin\Unsuccessful_Be an Angel: 62 – 64.
63 Berlin\Unsuccessful_Be an Angel: 33 – 33.
64 Cologne\Education_Rheinflanke: 31 – 31.
65 Cologne\Vulnerable groups_Agisra: 28 - 28; Cologne\Education_Rheinflanke: 32 – 32.
66 Cologne\Employment_Chance+: 31 – 31; Cologne\Social Assistance_Auszugsmanagement: 6 – 6.

profit activities. Along with generating additional income, working with (or sometimes establishing) for-profit entities can provide potential work-places to the clients of employment NPOs (e.g. the cooperation between Xiezhi and Alibaba and other regional firms), venues for education and training (e.g. the cooperation between Bridge and Vivantes), or places to live (such as Refugio's cohabitation house).[67] A third function of such set-ups is to foster networking and exchange among clients (such as the Rhe-inflanke and Refugio cafés). Sometimes this type of cooperation fulfils more than one function, such as Be an Angel's "Kreuzberger Himmel" restaurant which is a venue both for generating income and training the NPO's clients). Xiezhi specialised in big data technology and set up its own business. The firm uses big data to facilitate more efficient and effective matching between the country's job advertisements and the graduates of its universities,[68] thereby generating income, promoting its connection with universities throughout China, and solving the problem of matching talent and job opportunities.

(4) Ensuring Access to Expert Knowledge for the Provision of Services

Probably the most widespread function of NPO networks is to have ex-perts at hand for the provision of services. These experts might be lawyers, instructors, or other experts who are willing to share their knowledge and skills with the NPO's clients. Dinghe, for example, maintains contact with fifteen public welfare organisations in the 'Guangzhou Street Friends Care Service Alliance' to provide training in handicraft production and legal consultation for vagrants and beggars.[69] The teachers at Beida College come from their "teaching resources network", which consists of fifty-four colleges and universities "including Peking University, Renmin University of China, Zhejiang University, Sun Yat-sen University, and South China

---

67 Refugio is not profit-oriented, but generates some rental income: While the staff of the Refugio house is paid by the *Stadtmission,* which also owns the building, the inhabitants either pay their rents from earned incomes or have their housing costs covered by public entities (e.g. the job centres) if they are unemployed or if their incomes are insufficient to cover their living expenses (Berlin\Social Assis-tance_Refugio: 19 – 21).

68 Hangzhou_en\Employment_Xiezhi: 54 – 54.

69 Guangzhou_en\Vulnerable Groups_Dinghe Social Workers: 19 – 19.

University of Technology".[70] For its HaPiEnd project, the Agisra NPO connects its clients (refugee women) with "motivated craftswomen or volunteers and provides the necessary materials and tools" to help them renovate their flats before moving in.[71] Kein Abseits recruits students from Berlin universities to mentor young refugees and help them with their school homework and in communications with the authorities.[72] Auszugsmanagement, which originally focused on finding and renting accommodation for refugees, discovered that its clients often need further assistance and counselling. It therefore set up a network of related "public institutions, social organisations and welcome initiatives" that can provide professional assistance.[73] Although this is a tendency throughout the two countries investigated, we found that Chinese NPOs are often closely connected to universities and also involved in research projects, which applies to only some of the German NPOs in our sample.[74]

(5) Functioning as an Information Platform in their Field of Expertise (the Internet, Social Media, etc.)

Because NPOs accumulate considerable knowledge, skills and contacts in their day-to-day work, these organisations naturally tend to set up their own information platforms or even establish their own think tanks. This is especially true for China, where the NPOs in our sample very often had close connections to academic institutions and were often initiated by intellectuals. Superior Power, for instance, set up "the Private Think Tank for Social Construction in Guangdong" on issues of government, philanthropy, women and corporations.[75] GZ Lawyers Association uses online platforms to provide innovative legal aid, "including legal counselling, legal publicizing, and legal training". With this technology, and especially

---

70 Guangzhou_en\Education_Beida College: 20 – 20; Guangzhou_en\Education_Beida College: 56 – 56.
71 Cologne\Vulnerable groups_Agisra: 37 – 37.
72 Berlin\Education_Kein Abseits_Berlin: 41 – 41.
73 Cologne\Social Assistance_Auszugsmanagement: 73 – 73.
74 Kein Abseits! is no exception to this observation because its existing connections to Berlin's universities serve no scientific purposes but rather the recruitment of mentors for the education services offered by this NPO.
75 Guangzhou_en\Employment_Superior Power: 22 – 22.

mobile apps like WeChat, more clients can be reached and more information disseminated in more effective and efficient manners than offline.[76]

In short, German and Chinese NPOs make ample use of networks and the associated knowledge and skills in order to raise their visibility (and thereby increase both public trust and income from donations), ensure access to vital information for their work, collaborate with for-profit enterprises, and secure access to expertise needed for their manifold services, as well as to build platforms through which to share the information they accumulate in their projects.

2. Exchange Condition: Funding Uncertainty

Jones et al. also found evidence that organisations build networks to mitigate the transaction costs of "demand uncertainty". In the cases they investigated, such uncertainty would occur for example when the many companies involved in producing movies for the film industry went through periods of uncertainty concerning subsequent commissions. We find that the NPOs in our sample actually do not face demand uncertainty simply because the demand for their services is overwhelming. However, there is an aspect of *funding* uncertainty that affects the NPOs in our sample similarly.

The problem for most of the NPOs is not so much whether they can get contracts but rather for how long, because access to public funds requires a constant process of application and reapplication.[77] Another funding-related problem in some cases is that it can be limited to certain areas. Chance +, for example, found during one project phase that their clients needed a certain type of counselling. So they changed part of the project to meet this demand but were not allowed to transfer the corresponding part of the budget.[78] We found that in such situations the NPOs in our sample resorted to networks, similarly to the supplier companies in the film industry. Many of the reports in our sample tell of networking with potential funders, both in China and in Germany.[79] Usually the NPOs have to con-

---

76 Guangzhou_en\Social Assistance_GZ Lawyers Association: 52 – 52.
77 Berlin\Employment_Bridge: 111 – 111; Berlin\Unsuccessful_Be an Angel: 18 – 18.
78 Cologne\Employment_Chance+: 88 – 88.
79 For example: Hangzhou_en\Employment_Xiezhi: 54 – 54; Berlin\Employment_Bridge: 110 – 110; Guangzhou_en\Education_Beida College: 61 – 61; Cologne\Vulnerable groups_Agisra: 56 – 56; Cologne\Education_Rheinflanke: 69 – 69.

tact a number of different funders in order to conduct one project. Rhein-flanke runs part of its projects with funds from the European Union and other parts from different departments on different levels of government.[80] Kein Abseits receives public funding for 30 per cent of its work and needs to solicit the rest of its funds from other sources.[81] In some cases, it takes years to secure a commitment from local governments to fund certain projects or programmes.[82] Administrative requirements for NPOs applying for public funding can include reporting requirements that may have an impact on their work.[83] In some cases the requirements for certain licences to prove their capabilities can also mean additional expenditure that the NPOs cannot afford.[84] Some NPOs in China, however, seem to be confident of long-term funding once they have gone through and succeeded in the competitive bidding process. This seems to be particularly true for those NPOs that take over government functions, such as Dinghe and Superior Power.

In short, although the NPOs see a high demand for their services, most of them face difficult funding situations. Cooperation within networks helps them to secure funding by establishing reciprocal relationships and connections on a long-term basis.

3. Exchange Conditions: Task Complexity

Another similarity between the NPOs in our sample and the groups researched by Jones et al. is the fact that their tasks are highly complex. Helping to integrate migrants and refugees poses challenges to local governments. Complexity occurs because of: (1) the high numbers of people and parties involved, such as the high numbers of refugees in Germany and migrants in China requiring assistance; (2) the complex problems that require complex solutions, e.g. housing problems sometimes entail psychological problems, as shown by the case of Auszugsmanagement; (3) the generally scattered nature of the resources needed to solve these problems, including volunteers, experts, potential landlords and employers, as well as funds and media support.

---

80 Cologne\Education_Rheinflanke: 42 – 44; Cologne\Education_Rheinflanke: 55 – 55.
81 Cologne\Employment_Chance+: 59 – 59.
82 Berlin\Employment_Bridge: 112 – 112.
83 Berlin\Employment_Bridge: 112 – 112.
84 Berlin\Unsuccessful_Be an Angel: 37 – 37.

Although the target groups and the political, legal and social backgrounds differ between China and Germany, some of the challenges are similar. And the NPOs, again, turn to networks to deal with them.

(1) High Numbers of People and Parties Involved

One challenge is the generally large number of parties involved—target groups, experts and funders have all to be approached in a coordinated way. The numbers of people involved in China are much higher than those in Germany. The organisations use their networks in responding to this challenge. NPOs incorporated into networks themselves can organise large numbers of helpers to address these challenges. The two above-mentioned lawyers' associations in China and the Bridge and Chance+ networks in Germany are examples of this strategy.

(2) The Problems to be Solved are Complex and Demand Complex Solutions

The examples of the employment NPOs and their solutions show how many different tasks, areas of expertise and people are needed to facilitate employment for newly arrived refugees in Germany or migrants in China. In addition to potential employers, these include specialists in temporary housing as well as language, professional and other instructors. Again, as seen above, the NPOs utilise their extensive networks to provide multi-faceted solutions.

(3) The Resources for Solving the Problems are Scattered

Similarly, networks are needed because there is usually no single source that satisfies all the different requirements for a given problem. The section on asset specificity above showed how NPOs build networks to access expertise, knowledge and personnel that cannot be acquired from one specific source or provider.

To conclude, networking is a trend observed in all our cases in Germany and China. Organisations use networks to connect and cooperate in relationships that are usually not governed by contracts to deal with the high demands on their skills and knowledge (asset specificity), the uncertainty of their funding and the complexity of their tasks, thereby ensuring access to the greatest possible number of sources to help them solve pressing problems in their societies.

6 Conclusion

In this study we examined characteristics of and rationales behind state–NPO cooperation. Basing our work on a qualitative analysis of field research reports on nineteen German and Chinese cases of NPOs working in the field of migration we began with an analysis of the outsourcing activities by local governments in China and Germany that revealed many parallels but also some fundamental differences. In analysing our case studies, we found outsourcing of public services in the sense of Salamon's third-party government approach to be a practice in most of the German and Chinese cases in our sample. The cases show outsourcing characteristics across different relationship types, countries and policy areas. Seven (three Chinese and four German) of the cases analysed even display the transfer of administrative responsibilities from local governments to NPOs and show intense involvement by the NPOs in governance processes. In the German cases, less successful outsourcing structures in the third-party government sense correspond with less formalised forms of cooperation. In the Chinese cases, outsourcing structures appear to be negatively affected by an asymmetric power relationship that favours the government. With regard to the rationales behind local governments outsourcing services, the data from our sample showed that those in Germany turned to NPOs to complement existing services, while those in China outsource services that would otherwise not be offered at all. Outsourcing therefore improves the efficiency and effectiveness of public service provision in the German cases and facilitates the efficacy of public service provision in China. This finding underscores the observation that China's development model has long departed from the socialist idea of the state being responsible for all areas of society. In a way, the state in China is willing to outsource some of its responsibilities to a high degree while maintaining ultimate control, while in Germany's social market economy many responsibilities remain in the state's hands and local governments seem to prefer to solve social problems in a cooperative manner with NPOs. In light of this first finding, these insights show that an authoritarian state is not necessarily a caring state.

Second, our analysis of NPO networking behaviour was based on the theory of network governance proposed by Jones and her colleagues. We showed that all the German and Chinese NPOs in our sample used networking to overcome the difficulties in their working environments, which are characterised mainly by asset specificity, funding uncertainty, and task complexity. We identified four types of networking, namely NPOs that are themselves organised as networks (sometimes at the request of the local government such as Chance+ and Bridge), stakeholder networks, networks excluding government agents and networks in which the state plays a dominant role. Given the authoritarian political system of China our data demonstrated that many (but not all!) of the Chinese NPOs in our sample were embedded in a network with a dominant role played by the local government. At the same time, almost all the German and Chinese NPOs decided to include government actors in their networks which helps to ensure congruence of general concepts on how to solve the social issues at hand. Outsourcing and networking are similar strategies of local governments and NPOs in China and Germany—despite all the obvious differences. Although the state clearly plays a more dominant role in authoritarian China, we were able to show that local states and societal actors in both China and Germany can choose among diverse —rather than uniform—strategies to tackle pressing social issues.

References

Altrock, Uwe and Kunze, Ronald (eds.) (2016). *Stadterneuerung und Armut. Jahrbuch Stadterneuerung 2016*. Wiesbaden: Springer VS Verlag für Sozialwissenschaften.

Bevir, Mark. (2012). *Governance: A Very Short Introduction*. Oxford: Oxford University Press.

Bode, Ingo and Taco Brandsen (2014). "State-third Sector Partnerships: A short overview of key issues in the debate", *Public Management Review*, 16:8: 1055–1066.

Cai, Yang and Zhengkui Liu (2015). "Poverty and Health: Children of Rural-to-Urban Migrant Workers in Beijing, China", *Social Indicators Research*, 123:2: 459–477.

Costen, Jennifer M. (1998). "A Model and Typology of Government-NGO Relationships", *Nonprofit and Voluntary Sector Quarterly*, 27:3: 358–382.

Emerson, Kirk and Tina Nabatchi (2015). *Collaborative Governance Regimes*. Washington, DC: Georgetown University Press.

Evers, Adalbert (2011). »Wohlfahrtsmix im Bereich sozialer Dienste", in Adalbert Evers, Rolf G. Heinze and Thomas Olk (eds.) *Handbuch Soziale Dienste*, Wiesbaden: VS Verlag für Sozialwissenschaften, 265–283.

Freise, Matthias and Annette Zimmer (2019). "Zivilgesellschaft und Wohlfahrtsstaat in Deutschland: Eine Einführung." In Matthias Freise and Annette Zimmer (eds.) *Zivilgesellschaft und Wohlfahrtsstaat im Wandel. Akteure, Strategien und Politikfelder*, Wiesbaden: VS Verlag für Sozialwissenschaften, 3–5.

Freise, Matthias and Annette Zimmer (2019). "Zivilgesellschaft und Wohlfahrtsstaat in Deutschland: Ein kurzer Ausblick." In Matthias Freise and Annette Zimmer (eds.) *Zivilgesellschaft und Wohlfahrtsstaat im Wandel. Akteure, Strategien und Politikfelder*, Wiesbaden: VS Verlag für Sozialwissenschaften, 395–402.

Granovetter, Mark S. (1992). "Problems of explanation in economic sociology." In Nitin Nohria and Robert G. Eccles (eds.) *Networks and organizations: Structure, Form, and Action*, Boston: Harvard Business School Press, 25–56.

Hasmath, Reza and Jennifer Y.J. Hsu (eds.) (2015). *NGO Governance and Management in China*. London and New York: Routledge.

Heberer, Thomas (2006). »China – Entwicklung zur Zivilgesellschaft", *Aus Politik und Zeitgeschichte: Beilage zur Wochenzeitung Das Parlament*, 49, 20–29.

Hildebrandt, Timothy (2013). *Social Organizations and the Authoritarian State in China*. Cambridge and others: Cambridge University Press.

Hilton, Isabel (2013). "The return of Chinese civil society." In Sam Geall (ed.) *China and the Environment. The Green Revolution*, New York: Zed Books Ltd., 1–14.

Hood, Christopher (1991). "A Public Management for all Seasons". *Public Administration*, 69:1, 3–19.

Jing, Yijia (2015). "Between Control and Empowerment: Governmental Strategies towards the Development of the Non-profit Sector in China", *Asian Studies Review*, 39:4, 589–608.

Jing, Yijia and Yefei Hu (2017). "From Service Contracting to Collaborative Governance: Evolution of Government–Nonprofit Relations", *Public Administration and Development*, 37, 191–202.

Jones, Candace and William S. Hesterly and Stephen P. Borgatti, (1997). "A General Theory of Network Governance: Exchange Conditions and Social Mechanisms", *Academy of Management Review*, 22:4, 911–945.

Kang, Xiaoguang 康晓光 and Heng Han 恒韩 (2005). "分类控制：当代中国大陆国家与社会关系研 [*The system of differential controls: A study of the state–society relation in contemporary China*]. 社会学研究 [Sociological Studies] 20:6, 73–89.

Kang, Xiaoguang and Heng Han (2008). "The State-Society Relationship in Contemporary China", *Modern China*, 34:1, 36–55.

Kapucu, Naim and Qian Hu (2020). *Network Governance. Concepts, Theories, and Applications*. New York and London: Routledge.

Ketels, Anja (2019). "Migrant Integration as a Challenge for Local Governments and Social Organizations in China and Germany – Policy Traditions and Integration Measures in Guangzhou, Hangzhou, Berlin and Cologne", *LoGoSO Research Papers*, Nr. 8. Online available at https://refubium.fu-berlin.de/handle/fub188/24154.

Levy, Katja (2020). "Local Public Administration and Social policy in Germany and China", *LoGoSO Research Papers* Nr 5. Online available at https://refubium.fu-berlin.de/handle/fub188/17676.

Levy, Katja and Knut Benjamin Pissler (2020). *Charity with Chinese Characteristics. Chinese Charitable Foundations between the Party-state and Society.* Cheltenham: Edward Elgar.

Ma, Qingyu 马庆钰 and Hong Liao 鸿廖 (2015). 中国社会组织发展战略 [*National Strategy of Promoting the Development of China's Social Organizations*]. Beijing: Social Sciences Academic Press.

Najam, Adil. (2000). "The Four-C's of Third Sector–Government Relations. Cooperation, Confrontation, Complementarity, and Co-optation", *Nonprofit Management & Leadership*, 10:4, 375–396.

Saich, Tony (2000). "Negotiating the state: The development of social organizations in China", *The China Quarterly*, 161, 124–41.

Salamon, Lester (1995). *Partners in Public Service. Government-Nonprofit Relations in the Modern Welfare State.* Baltimore and London: The Johns Hopkins University Press.

Salamon, Lester (1987). "Of Market Failure, Voluntary Failure, and Third-Party Government: Toward a Theory of Government-Nonprofit Relations in the Modern Welfare State", *Nonprofit and Voluntary Sector Quarterly*, 16:1–2, 29–49.

Salamon, Lester (2011). "The New Governance and the Tools of Public Action: An Introduction", *Fordham Urban Law Journal*, 28:5, 1611–1674.

Salamon, Lester M. and Stefan Toepler (2015). "Government-Nonprofit Cooperation. Anomaly or Necessity?" *Voluntas*, 26, 2155–2177.

Schmitter, Philippe C. (1974). "Still the Century of Corporatism?" *The Review of Politics*, 36:1, 85–131.

Teets, Jessica (2014). *Civil Society under Authoritarianism. The China Model.* New York: Cambridge University Press.

Unger, Jonathan and Anita Chan (1995). "China, Corporatism, and the East Asian Model. The Australian Journal of Chinese Affairs, 33 (January), 29–53.

Wang, Qun and Xiaoguang Kang (2018). "China's Nonprofit Policymaking in the New Millennium", *Nonprofit Policy Forum*, 9:1, 1–4.

Wang, Weinan and Holly Snape (2018). "Government Service Purchasing from Social Organizations in China: An Overview of the Development of a Powerful Trend", *Nonprofit Policy Forum*, 9:1.

Young, Dennis R. (2000). "Alternative models of government-nonprofit sector relations: theoretical and international perspectives", *Nonprofit and Voluntary Sector Quarterly*, 29:1, 149–172.

Zimmer, Annette. (2010). "Third Sector-Government Partnerships". In Rupert Taylor (ed.) *Third Sector Research*, New York: Springer, 201–218.

Appendix

The Chinese cases

NPO name	City	Policy area	NPO founding date	Type and registration administrative level	Cooperation project name / start date	Project funding
广东北达经贸专修学院 Guangdong Beida Economic and Trade College (Beida College)	Guangzhou	Education	1999	Private non-enterprise unit (民办非企业单位), registered at provincial level	University Dream of Migrant Workers / 2010	Government funding, tuition fees, tuition reduction by Peking University
广州市黄埔区优势力社会工作发展中心 Superior Power Social Work Development Center (Superior Power)	Guangzhou	Employment	2011	Private non-enterprise unit (民办非企业单位), registered at district level	Social Work Service Project for Migrant Workers in the Super Large Towns of Huadu District / 2013	Government purchase of services
广州市律师协会 Guangzhou Lawyers Association (GZ Lawyers Association)	Guangzhou	Social assistance	1988	Social group (社会团体), registered at municipal level	Guangzhou Laborers' Rights and Interests Legal Aid Project / 2013	Membership fees (98%), government subsidies, social donations, operating income
广州市鼎和社会工作服务中心 Guangzhou Dinghe Social Work Service Center (Dinghe)	Guangzhou	Vulnerable groups	2013	Private non-enterprise unit (民办非企业单位), registered at district level	Project to Serve Vagrants and Beggars / 2014	Government purchase of services

NPO name	City	Policy area	NPO founding date	Type and registration administrative level	Cooperation project name / start date	Project funding
关爱环卫工人志愿服务队 Volunteer Service for Sanitation Workers (Sanitation Workers)	Guangzhou	Unsuccessful case	2013	Not registered	Volunteer Service for Sanitation Workers / 2013	Funding by the local sanitation station
杭州市慈善总会杭州网义工分会 Hangzhou Net Volunteer Branch of Hangzhou Charity Federation (HZ Net)	Hangzhou	Education	2005	Social group (社会团体), registered at municipal level	"Little Migratory Birds" summer camp / 2006	Private funding by the founder and by enterprises, infrastructure support from the government
浙江携职专修学院 Zhejiang Xiezhi Vocational College (Xiezhi)	Hangzhou	Employment	2008	Private non-enterprise unit (民办非企业单位), registered at municipal level	Job-seeking station for migrant workers, 2017	Private funding from the founder, foundations and government, operating income
杭州律师协会 Hangzhou Lawyers Association (HZ Lawyers Association)	Hangzhou	Social assistance	1991	Social group (社会团体), registered at municipal level	Action for the Protection of Migrant Workers' Rights and Interests / 2018	Membership fees, government funding, social donations, income from legal services
杭州市下城区起点益行社会工作发展中心 Qidian Yixing Social Work Development Center (Qidian Yixing)	Hangzhou	Vulnerable groups	2016	Private non-enterprise unit (民办非企业单位), registered at district level	Community integration project for elderly migrants / 2016	Government purchase of services
草根之家 Home of the Grassroots (Grassroots)	Hangzhou	Unsuccessful case	2006	Not registered	Cultural Center for Migrant Workers (X Service Station) / 2010	Corporate sponsorship, Oxfam fund support, government funding

The German cases

NPO name	City	Policy area	NPO founding date	Type of organisation	Cooperation project name / start date	Project funding
Kein Abseits! e.V. (Kein Abseits)	Berlin	Education	2011	Association	Mentoring programme for refugees / 2016	Government funding, private sources, donations, membership fees
Bridge network (Bridge)	Berlin	Employment	1986 Arbeit und Bildung e.V.: 1986 / network of various organisations	Various organisations	Bridge Bleiberecht / 2014	ESF Integration Guideline (*ESF-Integrationsrichtlinie Bund*): European Social Fund (ESF), Federal Ministry for Labour and Social Affairs, and Berlin Senate administration
Berliner Stadtmission/ Refugio (Refugio)	Berlin	Social assistance	1877	Association under the umbrella of the Protestant Church	Refugio / 2015	Berliner Stadtmission (mix of grants and subsidies, membership fees, operating income), project operating income, case-by-case government support
AWO Kreisverband Südost (AWO)	Berlin	Vulnerable groups	1919 AWO, 1994 AWO Kreisverband Südost	Association under the umbrella of AWO Bundesverband (federal association)	AWO Women's Counseling Center / 1990s	Funding by the senate administration
Be an Angel e.V. (Be an Angel)	Berlin	Unsuccessful case	2015	Association	Be an Angel / 2015	Private donations, sustaining members, fundraising campaigns
RheinFlanke gGmbH (Rheinflanke)	Cologne	Education	2006/2007	Private limited liability company with public benefit status	Project Hope / 2015	Asylum, migration and integration fund / European Union and the Federal Ministry for Labour and Social Affairs, operating income

NPO name	City	Policy area	NPO founding date	Type of organisation	Cooperation project name / start date	Project funding
Chance+ Netzwerk Flüchtlinge und Arbeit (Chance+)	Cologne	Employment	Caritasverband e.V.: 1897/ network of various organisations	Various organisations	Chance+ Network for Refugees and Employment / 2014	ESF Integration Guideline (*ESF-Integrationsrichtlinie Bund*): European Social Fund (ESF), Federal Ministry for Labour and Social Affairs, and Cologne Senate administration
Auszugsmanagement	Cologne	Social assistance	Cologne Refugee Council: 1984/ network of various organisations	Various organisations	Projekt Auszugsmanagement/ 2011	City administration
AGISRA e.V. (Agisra)	Cologne	Vulnerable groups	1993	Association	Activities for refugees / 2015	The state of North Rhine-Westphalia, city of Cologne, and the European Union, case-by-case funding by public administration, donations

Models of Cooperation between Local Governments and Social Organisations in Germany and China: Towards a Categorisation of the LoGoSO Models

Anja Ketels and Katja Levy

1 Introduction

LoGoSO stands for Local Governments (LoGo) and Social Organizations (SO) and is the short title of the comparative research project "Models of Co-operation between Local Governments and Social Organizations in Germany and China – Migration: Challenges and Solutions". In the course of the research project, nineteen case studies in four German and Chinese cities were conducted to analyse the cooperation between local governments and social organisations in services provision for asylum seekers in Germany and for migrant workers in China[1]. This contribution draws on these case studies and the investigations in this volume to move towards a categorisation of the cooperation models identified in the nineteen cases (LoGoSO models). With this article, we wish to contribute to earlier debates on the cooperation between local governments and social organisations by proposing a typology for state–SO cooperation. Such a typology may be useful for assessing the different types of relations easily and also for comparing them across different cultural and political backgrounds. Our starting point is the multidimensional typology by Jennifer Coston[2] (1998). In the course of applying this typology to the German and Chinese cases of the LoGoSO project, we adapted the taxonomy to accommodate both the German and the Chinese cases. By adapting the model, mainly in the dimensions of power balance and linkage between the organisations and the government, we are able to point out some important differences

---

1 A more detailed account of the contents and methods of the research project is provided in the introduction to this volume.
2 Coston uses the term non-governmental organisation (NGO) in her typology, while the LoGoSO project and this article work with the term social organisation (SO) as a common term in the Chinese context. In this article, the terms are used interchangeably to describe organisations which are non-profit and non-state in nature.

between German and Chinese state–SO cooperation. These observations go beyond the mere question of the dependency/autonomy of SOs on and from the state, which is often the centre of attention when discussing the third sector, particularly in non-democratic political systems. In this way, we also hope to contribute to the differentiation of knowledge on the People's Republic of China (PRC) in a more general sense.

The analyses of the case studies in this collection have investigated different aspects of the forms of cooperation: Zimmer and Grabbe as well as Ma et al. studied the administrative framework, institutional background, traditions of and challenges posed by the cooperation projects in the two different countries. Lovelady and Grabbe analysed the German cases from a new public governance perspective. Levy and Ketels identified similarities to and differences between the cooperation modes in the different constellations in Germany and China, focusing on the forms in which the cooperation modes answer to particular challenges for the actors involved. The studies have investigated, on the one hand, the challenges for local governments in providing services and integrating migrants, and, on the other hand, the challenges for SOs in fulfilling the quality requirements of the government agencies while sustaining their unique organisational identity and goals in the relationship. To complement this research, in this article, we identify and describe general patterns of government–SO cooperation in our two-country sample.

In the next section, we first provide an overview of earlier theoretical attempts at categorising state–SO relations and explain why we consider Jennifer Coston's typology a suitable theoretical starting point for categorising the LoGoSO models. Section 3 subsequently presents the nineteen cases of SO–government cooperation in the LoGoSO project with special regard to the characteristics of the cooperation mode. In section 4, we explain how we operationalised Coston's typology for this study and analyse the LoGoSO cases within this framework. Thereupon, in section 5, we apply and adopt Coston's original typology to the case studies and discuss the results and implications of the adapted typology.

2 Typologies of Government–NGO Relationships

In a review of the "empirical, theoretical and exploratory or polemical literature that has examined relationships between government agencies and non-state providers (NSPs) of basic services", Kelly Teamey provides a comprehensive overview of different typologies of state–NGO relationships. She distinguishes between three kinds of models of state–SO cooperation:

discourse models, continuum models and multidimensional models—in order of their complexity (Teamey 2007: 54). Discourse models, such as those by Skelcher et al. 2004 and Welle (2001), are mainly concerned with the question of how the two sides of the state–SO relationship frame their particular mode of cooperation. Continuum models, such as those by Farrington and Lewis (1993) and Wamai (2004) are described by Teamy as simple models with usually only one or two dimensions for the description of cooperation. The multi-dimensional models, such as those by Najam (2000), Young (2000) and Coston (1998), are the most complex (and also most widely cited) ones. Najam's model distinguishes between four strategic choices of state–SO cooperation, i.e. cooperation, complementarity, co-optation and confrontation (the "four Cs"). Young's perspective refers to economic theory and focuses on comparative advantage. He distinguishes between three slightly different functions of the non-profit sector, i.e. supplementary, complementary or adversarial (Teamy 2007: 54 ff.). Coston's suggestion on how to describe the relationships is more complex, as we will describe in more detail below.

Since the LoGoSO research project aims to identify models of cooperation between the state and SOs in service provision, we are interested in the factors that affect this cooperation. We are particularly interested in finding a way to categorise them, taking the political systems into consideration since they provide the setting for the relationships. The state's attitude towards non-profits and the role of power in the relationships are important for our project, as the two country cases, Germany and China, are very different and make comparisons challenging. Coston's model is best suited as a framework for such comparisons for a number of reasons: it explicitly considers different government attitudes concerning institutional plurality, in other words, attitudes concerning SOs' right to existence; it considers the distribution of power in the relationships, which is an important factor in the observations of the cases in our sample; it identifies eight types of cooperation and thereby acknowledges a high degree of heterogeneity in relationships; and it has been developed for general and rapid assessment against the background of different contexts. Therefore, we chose Coston's model to categorise the types of cooperation we found in the LoGoSO project cases. Below, we describe Coston's typology in more detail.

Jennifer M. Coston (1998) developed her "model and typology of government–NGO relationships" to enable actors in the third sector to identify the most productive types of relationships for particular contexts (Coston 1998: 358). The typology distinguishes between eight types of state–NGO relationships: repression, rivalry, competition, contracting, third-party government, cooperation, complementarity, and collaboration. The types are defined in four dimensions: the government's acceptance of or resistance to institutional pluralism, the level of government–NGO linkage, the relative power in the relationship and the degree of formality in the relationship. Coston illustrated the eight cooperation types by arranging them on three parallel continua (ranging from asymmetrical power relationship to symmetrical power relationship, from informal to formal relationships, and from resistance to acceptance of institutional pluralism by the government) (see Figure 1).

Coston's typology proposes a linear increase in asymmetry in the power relationship. It argues that the exercise of government power is stronger in authoritarian regimes. Coston also suggests that in authoritarian regimes there is little to no formal linkage between NGOs and the government (Coston 1998: 363). She describes three categories of cooperation in which power relationships are asymmetrical:

- *Repression* refers to a lack of acceptance of institutional pluralism, no linkage between organisation and government and a strong power balance in favour of the government. This relationship can be formal or informal. Government support and the legal framework are not supportive for NGOs. The relationship is a one-way relationship.
- *Rivalry* is very similar to repression but can also take the form of a two-way relationship.
- *Competition* is similar to repression and rivalry but is always informal and government policy is less hostile towards NGOs. NGOs and governments may compete for political, economic or potential benefits. (Coston 1998: 361).

Figure 1: Coston's typology of government–NGO relationships (Coston, 1998)

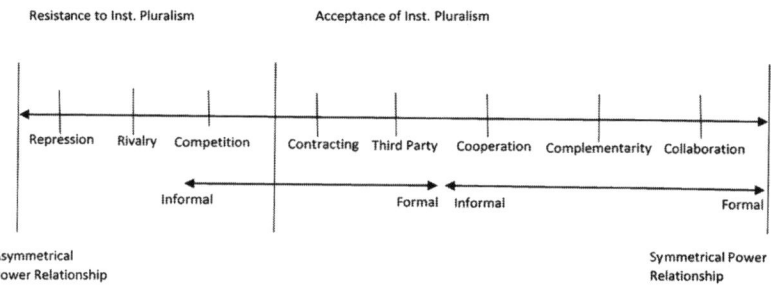

The government–NGO relationship types in liberal democracies in this model, on the other hand, are shaped by the acceptance of institutional pluralism and differ mainly in regard to the degree of formalisation and the intensity of linkage in the respective relationship:

- *Contracting* is based on a formal document and characterised by moderate to high linkage between the government and an NGO, the latter being involved in clearly specified services,
- *Third-party government* is similar to contracting; however, the formalisation can be more diverse than contracting, including e.g. loan guarantees or insurance. There is also a greater diversity in services,
- *Cooperation* is not formalised and might occur on a regular or ad hoc basis with low NGO–government linkage,
- Complementarity translates into a relationship where the NGO works almost on par with government entities in a relatively informal setting
- *Collaboration* characterises a mode of governance where there is no difference between the government and the non-profit service unit. It is highly formalised and might also result in a situation in which the NGO is thoroughly co-opted by the government (Coston 1998: 361–362).

Coston's typology has been applied by authors to a number of different case and actor groups. Most of the studies just mention the typology briefly or apply the typology as it is without adapting it further.[3] In their contribution to this volume, Lovelady and Grabbe show that Coston's typology is applicable to the German cases and covers the diversity in these relationships. Jennifer Y. J. Hsu has attempted to adapt the typology to China. In her studies of migrant NGOs in Beijing and Shanghai, she starts out with Coston's typology but then departs from this model and proposes a "layers and spaces framework" (Hsu 2012 and Hsu 2017). She finds that local states and NGOs engage in three kinds of relationships, i.e. *symbolic, asymmetric and strategic* relationships. *Symbolic* cooperation "refers to the state's acknowledgement and acceptance of the NGO and its work, possibly without a working relationship between the state and the NGO" (Hsu 2017, 39). Hsu finds that this kind of cooperation is the preferred pattern in relationships with governments on the municipal and central levels and serves to enhance the legitimacy of the respective administrative level. *Asymmetric relationship* refers to relations "in which the NGO, due to the power monopoly of the state, becomes dependent on the state to facilitate

---

3 See, for example, Katsongo 2012 and Wael 2019.

its work" (ibid.). Chinese district level governments seem to prefer this type of cooperation according to Hsu. And *strategic collaboration* "enables the state to make choices in its engagement with NGOs for the purpose of fulfilling certain goals, such as economic goals" (Hsu 2017, 8). This is a co-operation type found at the lowest administrative level in China, the level of street neighbourhoods and residential committees. Hsu holds that "[i]t is clear that neither [her] case study nor China itself fits so comfortably in [Coston's] continuum, and Chinese NGOs operate in an unfavourable institutional environment. However, various levels of the state have tacitly acknowledged the growing pluralism of social stakeholders" (Hsu 2017, 39, Ketels 2018).

In the following, we first present the LoGoSO cases and their cooperation modes and then explain how we think that Coston's model needs to be modified in order to be applicable for the categorisation of all the German and Chinese cases in our sample. In the overall attempt of the project to compare the cases of the two countries, applying the typology by providing general parameters of comparison proves to be a helpful tool in categorising the cases. As we will show in our analysis, we agree with Hsu that the model needs adaptation for Chinese cases. However, our adaptation departs less from the individual types of Coston's typology but modifies the fundamental conceptualisation of the continua used in her model and also suggests merging and adjusting the types.

3   The Cases of Local Government–SO Cooperation in Germany and China in the LoGoSO Project

The LoGoSO project examined cases of cooperative efforts between local government and SOs. The study focused on SOs that provided services for migrants in the policy areas of education, employment, social assistance (including legal aid), vulnerable groups as well as cases in which cooperation could not be achieved ("unsuccessful cases"). We chose the common issue area of migration in China and Germany because—despite the political, historical and cultural differences between the two countries—local governments face comparable challenges in integrating incoming migrants, which similarly leads to cooperation between local government and SOs. As for Germany, refugees and asylum seekers from war-ridden countries like Syria headed for the country in 2015. It was one of several migration periods in German history (see introduction and Gluns 2017 for details). China's cities' migrant workers travel from rural to urban areas within the country in search of better income and living conditions. They are tolerated by the government, who acknowledges the need for a large workforce for China's economic development. However, the migrant workers' integration into the social security system of the cities is determined by the household registration system, which binds people's households and social security provision to the place where they are born, and therefore hampers the migrant workers' access to social services in their target localities.

In both countries, local governments bear the responsibility for integrating the incoming people and they similarly engage in cooperation with SOs, which provide solutions to coping with these challenges (see the introduction to this volume). In all the cases in the sample—except those where cooperation did not succeed—we found that there is a willingness to cooperate from both the local governments and the SOs. However, the cooperation modes differ regarding their intensity, degree of formality and the power structures in the relationship as well as the rationales behind the tasks and their distribution.

The Chinese sample (see Table 1) encompasses different constellations: three cases where the government purchases certain services from the SO (*Superior Power, Dinghe, Qidian Yixing*), two cases where the project started as a bottom-up initiative by citizens and later evolved into a form of cooperation with the government (*Xiezhi, HZ Net*), one case where the SO and the local government jointly established a programme (*Beida College*), and two cases in which structure of the project and the SO are set up, managed and controlled by the government (*HZ Lawyers, GZ Lawyers*). The two cases in which cooperation did not succeed (*Sanitation Workers, Grassroots*) are characterised by a situation in which the government did not approve of the work of the SO and took over complete control of the project.

Table 1: The Chinese Cases

SO name	City	Policy field	Cooperation project name/ start date
广东北达经贸专修学院 Guangdong Beida Economic and Trade College (*Beida College*)	Guangzhou	Education	University Dream of Migrant Workers/ 2010
广州市黄埔区优势力社会工作发展中心 Superior Power Social Work Development Centre (*Superior Power*)	Guangzhou	Employment	Social Work Service Project for Migrant Workers in the Super Large Towns of Huadu District/ 2013
广州市律师协会 Guangzhou Lawyers Association (*GZ Lawyers*)	Guangzhou	Social assistance	Guangzhou Labourers' Rights and Interests Legal Aid Project/ 2013
广州市鼎和社会工作服务中心 Guangzhou Dinghe Social Work Service Centre (*Dinghe*)	Guangzhou	Vulnerable groups	Project to Serve Vagrants and Beggars/ 2014
关爱环卫工人志愿服务队 Volunteer Service for Sanitation Workers (*Sanitation Workers*)	Guangzhou	Unsuccessful case	Volunteer Service for Sanitation Workers/ 2013
杭州市慈善总会杭州网义工分会 Hangzhou Net Volunteer Branch of Hangzhou Charity Federation (*HZ Net*)	Hangzhou	Education	"Little Migratory Birds" summer camp/ 2006
浙江携职专修学院 Zhejiang Xiezhi Vocational College (*Xiezhi*)	Hangzhou	Employment	Job-seeking station for migrant workers, 2017
杭州律师协会 Hangzhou Lawyers Association (*HZ Lawyers*)	Hangzhou	Social assistance	Action for the Protection of Migrant Workers' Rights and Interests/ 2018
杭州市下城区起点益行社会工作发展中心 Qidian Yixing Social Work Development Centre (*Qidian Yixing*)	Hangzhou	Vulnerable groups	Community integration project for elderly migrants / 2016
草根之家 Home of the Grassroots (*Grassroots*)	Hangzhou	Unsuccessful case	Cultural Centre for Migrant Workers (X Service Station)/ 2010

Our cases in Germany (see Table 2) are generally characterised by more initiative and independence on the side of the SOs. While the cooperation in the Chinese cases is mostly dominated by stronger government control and supervision, the German cases tend to show examples of eye-level cooperation between SOs and the government. Most projects are bottom-up initiatives by the SOs that later evolved into cooperation with the government (*Kein Abseits, Refugio, AWO, HOPE, Auszugsmanagement, Agisra*).

Among these cases, three modes of cooperation developed into close and interconnected relationships between SOs and the government (*Kein Abseits, AWO, Auszugsmanagement*), while three cases remain largely autonomous and only cooperate on a case-to-case basis (*Refugio, Agisra, HOPE*). Exceptions are the two employment networks *Bridge* and *Chance+*, which developed in response to a call by the government and provide services within the framework of the federal government's integration programme. The case of unsuccessful cooperation in Germany (*Be an Angel*) started out as a grassroots initiative and works in a largely isolated manner, using the means of lobbying, advocacy and openly criticising the local government instead of collaborating with it in order to participate in policy-making.

Table 2: The German Cases

SO name	City	Policy field	Cooperation project name/ start date
Kein Abseits! e.V. (*Kein Abseits*)	Berlin	Education	Mentoring programme for refugees/ 2016
Bridge network (*Bridge*)	Berlin	Employment	Bridge Bleiberecht/ 2014
Berliner Stadtmission/ Refugio (*Refugio*)	Berlin	Social assistance	Refugio / 2015
AWO Kreisverband Südost (*AWO*)	Berlin	Vulnerable groups	AWO Women's Counselling Centre / 1990s
Be an Angel e.V. (*Be an Angel*)	Berlin	Unsuccessful case	Be an Angel/ 2015
RheinFlanke gGmbH (*HOPE*)	Cologne	Education	Project HOPE/ 2015
Chance+ Netzwerk Flüchtlinge und Arbeit (*Chance+*)	Cologne	Employment	Chance+ Network for Refugees and Employment/ 2014
Auszugsmanagement	Cologne	Social assistance	Projekt Auszugsmanagement/ 2011
AGISRA e.V. (*Agisra*)	Cologne	Vulnerable groups	Activities for refugees/ 2015

Having presented the main characteristics of the cases in the LoGoSO sample, we conduct an analysis of their cooperation types in the next section.

4 Analysis of the LoGoSO Cases

For the analysis of the cases, we operationalise Coston's model of state–SO relations according to its following four dimensions[4]:

- acceptance of plurality (whether the state accepts the existence of NGOs)
- linkage degree (how tight the linkage between the government and NGOs is)
- power symmetry (how far the power of government and that of the NGO are in symmetry)
- formality (how formally institutionalised the relations are).

While these dimensions work well with the German cases (as Lovelady and Grabbe have shown in their article in this collection), the model lacks applicability for the Chinese cases for the following reasons.

First, the model assumes that, in authoritarian states, the government generally does not accept plurality. This is actually the case for the many organisations in China that have not managed to register according to the legal rules applying to them, and thereby exist and operate illegally according to Chinese standards.[5] However, as the cases of cooperation in our sample show, in those cases where the organisations have legally registered and work within the legal framework, the state very much accepts plurality of providers of public services in China. In fact, the state does not only accept plurality, but also fosters cooperation in certain areas, as our samples in the area of service provision for migrants show.

Second, the degree of linkage between the government and an organisation is not expressive enough to understand the *quality of the linkage*. Linkage quality may entail how trustful the relationship is, how much and what kind of information is exchanged, or whether the government is willing to share or even transfer some of its own responsibilities to the organisation. E.g. in the case of Superior Power, the local government is willing

---

4 We extracted these dimensions from Coston's Figure 1 (1998, 361–362). Her typology includes two more dimensions: *government policy* (whether government policy is favourable regarding NGOs or not) and *relationship direction* (one- or two-way). However, only the first four dimensions have found their way into her final model (see our Figure 1 above or Coston's Figure 2, 363).

5 The reasons for organisations not being able to register range from professionalism related reasons, such as the organisations' lack of experience, professional skills or networks, to political reasons, such as the political sensitivity of the issue area, activities of the organisations or the character of their founder.

to transfer some public administration responsibilities to the organisation and also accepts its suggestions for further developing certain policies. In the cases of the networks Bridge and Chance+, SOs and the government even share the same employees, jointly coordinate their work and frequently consult each other.

Third, Coston assumes a negative correlation between government suppression and government acceptance of pluralism, which is connected to the linkage degree in the relationship. She argues that the power asymmetry is largest when institutional pluralism is not accepted and there is no linkage between the government and an SO. Relations with a strong government–NGO linkage on the other hand are understood to exist in a setting with more power symmetry. However, we find in our examples that for China, regardless of acceptance of or resistance to pluralism, there is actually a clear nexus between the degree of linkage in the relationship and repression or control. In other words, for the Chinese cases it can be stated that the closer a relationship gets the more power the local government has in the relationship with the SO.

Finally, and probably most obviously, we observe a stronger power position for the local government in their relationship with the SO in all the Chinese cases. While the state has a power advantage in liberal democracies as well, the power asymmetry is stronger in China. However, there are organisations, even in the PRC, which manage to maintain a certain degree of influence and independent decision-making power in their relationship with the local government. This is usually the case when the organisation is able to provide services or public goods that the state does not deliver but considers important. A very good example is Xiezhi, which, among many other things, provides a big data analysis service that is able to match the job advertisements of companies scattered on the Chinese internet with the student graduate information of Chinese universities. This service is able, at least according to our discussions with Xiezhi, to bring together jobs and graduates much more efficiently than any service offered by the various levels of government. Xiezhi can utilise the high interest of the universities and local governments in its services to gain considerate manoeuvring space and power in relation to their local government.

We therefore suggest the following adaptations to the Coston typology to make it applicable to cases in Western liberal democracies and, at the same time, in authoritarian states like China with its complex relationship between the government and SOs. We assume there is a general acceptance of institutional pluralism for legally established organisations in all kinds of political systems. In addition, we add the dimension of linkage quality to display some of Coston's specifications in the description of the different relationship types. The adapted four dimensions are as follows:

- *Power symmetry (PS)* describes the distribution of power between the government and an SO. While in government–SO relationships there is always a certain degree of power on the side of the government, a symmetric power relationship is a situation in which the SO has a power advantage that allows it to act without intrusions. An asymmetric power relationship on the other hand is characterised by a strong power advantage on side of the government, which grants it total control over the actions of the SO.
- *Formality (F)* stands for the formal regulation of the cooperation. Informal relationships exist when an SO and the government cooperate e.g. on a case-to-case basis without any formal agreement, while formal relationships are based on an agreement such as a cooperation contract, which clearly defines the role allocation and responsibilities of each party.
- *Linkage degree (LD)* relates to the intensity of interconnection in the relationship. In a relationship without any linkage, the government and SO have little contact and hardly relate to one another. A strong linkage on the contrary, characterises cooperation in which the government and an SO are completely interconnected and work on par with each other.
- *Linkage quality (LQ)* illustrates the quality of the exchanges in the cooperation by including factors such as mutual exchange of information, diversity of services or SO involvement in public administration. It varies from low linkage quality with limited valuable communication or only clearly specified areas of cooperation to many and sophisticated exchanges where the SO is involved in a variety of government responsibilities and might even participate in decision-making processes.

Table 3 shows the 19 LoGoSO cases with varying degrees of the four characteristics and specification of the four dimensions in each case, and sorts the cases into groups with similar characteristics. The cases in the table are arranged in the order of increasing degrees of formality, linkage degree and linkage quality.

Table 3: Coston's dimensions in the LoGoSO cases

Case	PS	F	LD	LQ
Be an Angel	0	0	0	0
Refugio	0	0.5	0.5	0.5
HZ Net	1	0.5	1	1
Xiezhi	1	0.5	1	1
Agisra	0.5	1	1	1
HOPE	1	1	1	1
Qidian Yixing	1.5	2	1.5	1
AWO	1	2	1.5	1
Superior Power	1.5	2	1.5	1.5
Dinghe	1.5	2	1.5	1.5
Kein Abseits	1	2	1.5	1.5
Home of Grassroots	2	2	2	1
Sanitation Workers	2	2	2	1
HZ Lawyers	2	2	2	1.5
GZ Lawyers	2	2	2	1.5
Auszugsmanagement	1.5	2	2	2
Beida College	1.5	2	2	2
Bridge	1.5	2	2	2
Chance+	1.5	2	2	2

Explanations:

PS=Power Symmetry (0=symmetric power relationship, 1=some power for SO, 2=asymmetric power relationship)

F=Formality (0=informal, 1=formal and informal/some formality, 2=formal)

LD=Linkage Degree (0=no linkage, 1=some linkage, 2=strong linkage)

LQ=Linkage Quality (0=low quality, 1=some quality, 2= high quality); the higher the quality the more information and responsibilities are shared in the relationship.

Grey shading: Chinese cases, No shading: German cases

The values in this table are not absolute, but relational estimates developed from the case descriptions.

The table illustrates that the state–SO relations in our sample in both countries showed varying degrees of formality, linkage degree and linkage quality. For all the Chinese cases, the power balance was clearly in favour of the government. While this comes as no surprise in the case of authoritarian China, it is remarkable that there are some organisations in that country that find ways of moving the power balance more in favour of the individual organisation to a certain degree. Our above-mentioned observation that there is a simultaneous increase in linkage degree and power balance in favour of the government, i.e. control from above, also shows itself in Table 3.

In trying to apply Coston's typology, we notice that Coston tried to conceptualise very similar subcategories. Although the intention was probably to be able to assess a great variety of differences, the result is actually that there are still more varieties when real world cases are analysed. We also notice that Coston's typology, although it is finer-grained than other models, is not nuanced enough to capture the many variations in real world cases. At the same time, her categories overlap, particularly in the following three groups: (1) repression, rivalry, competition; (2) cooperation, complementarity; (3) contracting, third-party government. A last observation while categorising our cases is that some Chinese cases form an additional type that is characterised by a very high degree of linkage, formality and strong power on the side of the government (the cases in question are HZ lawyers and GZ lawyers).

Using our empirical research as a basis, we therefore put forward three suggestions to further develop Coston's model to be applicable not only to Western liberal democratic countries but also to authoritarian states like China:

First, we suggest distinguishing between linkage degree and linkage quality, which was inherent in Coston's model but not explicit. This distinction captures the qualitative differences in the cooperation models better. As mentioned before, linkage quality refers to the extent the two partners in the relationship share information and responsibilities.

Second, we suggest merging some of Coston's types and adding one. With slightly broader types, a larger variety of cooperation relations can be captured. The newly arranged types are:

- *Competition.* Merges Coston's types of repression, rivalry and competition; characteristics: low degrees of formality, linkage and linkage quality with power advantage on the side of the SO.[6]

---

6 Differs from Coston's definition of competition in that the state does accept institutional pluralism and in the distribution of power.

- *Interaction.* Comprises what Coston calls cooperation and complementarity;[7] characteristics: balance between state and SO power, medium formality, medium linkage degree and linkage quality.
- *Outsourcing.* Comprises contracting and third-party government; characterised by a power relation that is either balanced or slightly to the advantage of the government, formality high, linkage degree and quality medium to high.[8]
- *GONGO.* This new type is a typical Chinese state–SO relationship is characterised by complete government power, high formality and linkage degree, as well as a medium to high linkage quality.
- *Collaboration.* This type is similar to Coston's collaboration type[9], which is characterised by a power relationship that is mostly in favour of the government, high formality, as well as high linkage degree and linkage quality.

Third, we observe a clear nexus between linkage degree, linkage quality, formality and power relations. The closer and more formal the relationship between the government and an SO gets, the more power advantage is on the side of the government. In order to take this nexus into consideration, we propose rearranging the categories in a new system of coordinates, with continua that capture the parallel increase in formality, linkage degree, linkage quality (on the x-axis) and the order of increasing state power in the relationship on the y-axis.[10]

After making these adaptions of Coston's model, we can now apply the new categories to the 19 cases in the LoGoSO project in the next chapter.

---

7 Differs with regard to power symmetry. There were no cases with a relationship type characterised by low formality and high linkage degree as suggested in Coston's complementarity.

8 Very similar to contracting and third-party government in Coston's model. In her model, the two categories differed mainly in linkage quality, with third-party government being characterised by more sharing of information and responsibilities in the relationship.

9 Differs from Coston's collaboration type with regard to power symmetry in that the power advantage is higher here for the government.

10 See Figure 2 below.

5 Categorising models of cooperation between local governments and social organisations in Germany and China

Using the adapted framework of analysis, the 19 cases can be grouped as follows:

(1) Competition

The German case of unsuccessful cooperation between the state and the SO Be an Angel fulfils the criteria of low formality, no linkage as well as full power advantage in favour of the state.

(2) Interaction

The cases in which the SO manages to retain considerable power in its relationship with the government, while maintaining a medium degree of linkage with some sharing of information and/or responsibility in formal or informal ways, belong to this group. For Germany, this categorisation is applicable to Refugio, Agisra and HOPE. The two Chinese cases HZ Net and Xiezhi also belong to this type.

(3) Outsourcing

This type includes those cases of SOs which maintain highly formalised, rather tightly linked relationships with their local governments. The governments have a clear power advantage but leave some decision-making power to the organisation, while sharing selected information and in some cases also certain public administration responsibilities with the SOs. Two German organisations, Kein Abseits and AWO, and three Chinese SOs, Superior Power, Dinghe and Qidian Yixing can be categorised as this type.

(4) GONGOs

Four Chinese relationships meet the criteria of a typical GONGO: HZ Lawyers, GZ Lawyers, Sanitation Workers and Home of Grassroots. This relationship is completely controlled and dominated by government power and characterised by high formality and linkage degree, as well as a medium to high linkage quality.

(5) Collaboration

The German cases Auszugsmanagement, Bridge and Chance+, and the Chinese Case Beida College belong in this group because they can be characterised as relationships with rather strong control mechanisms on the government's side, very formal relationships with high degrees in linkage and linkage quality, i.e. broad sharing of information and/or responsibilities.

Figure 2 shows the categorisation of the nineteen cases in the adapted typology.

Figure 2: Categorisation of the LoGoSO cases. Adapted from Coston's model of government–NGO relationships (Coston, 1998)

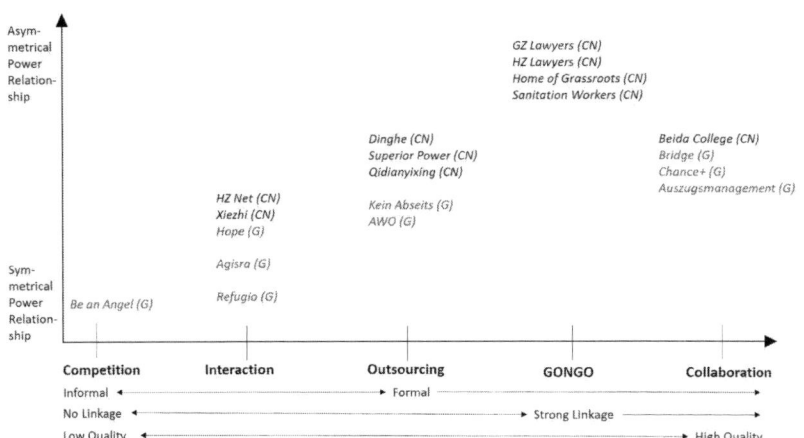

The illustration in Figure 2 reveals some particular observations from the comparison between the Chinese and German cases in the sample. In the German cases, the SOs work in an environment that is characterised by more power symmetry between the government and SOs, which generally grants more decision-making power to the SOs. The government is accepting of plurality, even in a competitive relationship type as the one with Be an Angel. As far as the linkage degree is concerned, the German cases vary strongly.

As for the Chinese cases, a general insight that was to be expected is the strong role of the state in the relationships. What is rather counter-intuitive is the finding that the Chinese government accepts the need for institutional plurality in service provision, although recent legislation on the third sector does, in part, put pressure on SOs. As discussed elsewhere (e.g. Levy 2018), the acceptance is, however, less broad than, for example, in Germany. There is a trend towards a high degree of formalisation in the state–SO relationships with fewer cases where the cooperation is relatively informal. Figure 2 illustrates the large variety we found among the Chinese cases, in linkage degree and variations in the power balance in the relations. It also shows that the Chinese state tends towards close cooperation forms that include information and/or responsibility sharing with the respective organisations and towards outsourcing that includes a high degree of information and/or responsibility sharing with the respective organisations.[11]

6 Conclusion

In this article, we propose a new typology of government–SO cooperation in order to facilitate assessment and comparison of state–SO relationships in liberal democratic and authoritarian settings despite the obvious cultural, historical, economic and political differences in these settings. The typology takes Jennifer Coston's typology of government–NGO relationships (1998) as its foundation but refines and adapts the individual types and also the relations between the types on the basis of the results of field research in Germany and China between 2016 and 2019. The new typology is now suitable for direct comparisons of the relationships, seeing their differences and similarities without neglecting their country-specific characteristics. This new typology may be useful for the assessment and comparison of more cases in more diverse country settings.

References

Coston, Jennifer M. (1998). "A Model and Typology of Government–NGO Relationships", *Non-profit and Voluntary Sector Quarterly*, 27:3, 358–382.

Farrington, J. and Bebbington, A (1993). *Reluctant Partners? Non-governmental organisations, the state and sustainable agricultural development*. London: Routledge.

Gluns, Danielle (2017). Report 4 "Current Migration Trends in Germany". Available online at: https://logosoprojectsite.files.wordpress.com/2017/02/t4-current-migration-trends-in-germany.pdf (last access: 17 January 2020).

Hsu, Jennifer (2012). "Layers of the Urban State: Migrant Organisations and the Chinese State", *Urban Studies*, 49:16, 3513–3530.

Hsu, Jennifer Y. J. (2017). *State of Exchange: Migrant NGOs and the Chinese Government*. Vancouver: UBC Press.

---

11 As is explicated in more detail in the introduction to this collection, the cases studied in this research project were selected carefully according to several selection criteria. The precondition for the majority of the cases (except the control group of cases with unsuccessful relations) was that the organisations had established working relationships with the government. Therefore, the many organisations in China (and Germany) that cannot cooperate with their government due to professional, legal or other reasons are not depicted in this typology. These organisations are beyond the scope of this study.

Katsongo, Kamathe (2012). "Partnership Modalities for the management of drinking water in poor urban neighbourhoods: The example of Kinshasa, Democratic Republic of Congo". In Robertson, Mélanie. *Sustainable Cities. Local Solutions in the Global South*. Ottawa and others: Practical Action Publishing, 113–132.

Ketels, Anja (2018). "Jennifer Y. J. Hsu: State of Exchange: Migrant NGOs and the Chinese Government (book review)", *Voluntas*, https://doi.org/10.1007/s11266-018-0034-7.

Levy, Katja (2018). "Boon or bane? The impact of two recent laws on civic organisations and their work in the People's Republic of China". Paper presented at the Annual Conference of the ISTR, Amsterdam.

Najam, Adil (2000). "The four C's of third sector – government relations: Cooperation, confrontation, complementarity and co-optation", *Nonprofit Management and Leadership*, 10:4, 375–396.

Skelcher, Chris (2004). "Hybrids: Implications of New Corporate Forms for Public Service Performance", Paper to the British Academy of Management Conference, Edinburgh.

Teamey, Kelly (2007). "Whose Public Action? Analysing Inter-sectoral Collaboration for Service Delivery Literature Review on Relationships between Government and Non-state Providers of Services", Working Paper of the International Development Department School of Public Policy, University of Birmingham.

Wael, Reem (2019). *Negotiating the Power of NGOs: Women's Legal Rights in South Africa*. Cambridge: Cambridge University Press.

Wamai, Richard G. (2004). "Recent International Trends in NGO Health System Organization, Development and Collaborations with Government in Transforming Health Care Systems: The Case of Finland and Kenya", Unpublished PhD doctoral dissertation, Department of Social Policy/Institute of Development Studies, University of Helsinki Finland.

Welle, Katharina (2001). "Contending discourses on 'Partnership'. A comparative analysis of the rural water and sanitation sector in Ghana", Occasional Paper, Water Issues Study Group, SOAS, University of London, September 2001.

Young, Dennis (2000). "Alternative models of government–nonprofit sector relations: theoretical and international perspectives", *Nonprofit and Voluntary Sector Quarterly*, 29:1, 149–172.

From the Perspective of Corporatism: A Comparative Analysis of the Relationship between Chinese and German Governments and their NPOs

Ma Qingyu , Xie Ju and Li Nan

1 Introduction

NPOs are made possible by social rights and, hence, constitute the basis of interactive relationships with the power of the state. Although in some countries NPOs have been around for a long time, the modern non-profit sector developed after World War II. Since then, the sector has enjoyed special acknowledgement in academic discussions that focus on the relationship between the state and society. In ancient Greece, Socrates (469 BC–399 BC), Plato (427 BC–347 BC) and Aristotle (384 BC–322 BC) believed in the intertwining of state power and civic life. In contrast, during the period of European enlightenment, the dualism of the state and society was stipulated by the political philosophy of those who advocated on behalf of the *supremacy of the state* (Niccolò Machiavelli, Jean Bodin, Thomas Hobbes, G. W. F. Hegel), and also by those who were in favour of the *supremacy of society* (John Locke, Adam Smith, Thomas Paine and Montesquieu) (Pang 2008, 65). Most recently, alongside the wave of democratisation after World War II, the United Nations promoted the global legalisation of the freedom of association through *the universal declaration of human rights* (1948). With the so-called "global association revolution" (Salamon 1994), non-profit organisations have flourished in developed countries and some developing countries since the 1970s.

Since 1978, the non-profit sector has also grown rapidly in China, attracting many scholars to study the relationship between the state and society. Since the theory of corporatism is directly related to the current situation in China, some scholars advocate that the approach is very useful for analysing the relationship between the state and social organisations (Pearson 1994, 31; Chen 2003, 176; Howell 2003, 19; Gu and Wang 2005, 155–175; Wang 2008, 151–156; Chen 2010, 30–43; Fan 2010, 159–176). Indeed, corporatism as a theoretical approach deserves special attention in China, a country in which there is a legacy of governmental and political power absorbing and penetration of society (Kang, Han et al. 2007, 116–128).

Also, Germany constitutes an interesting case for the study of government–NPO relations under the lens of corporatism (Zimmer 1999, Cui 2017, 69–75), particularly in the area of social or welfare service provision. Although faced with great challenges in global administrative reform since the 1980s, German NPOs active in the field of social service provision adapted to the changes in the environment (Henriksen et al. 2012). Since Germany's third sector has a corporatist tradition in that large umbrella associations took over an organising function for smaller social organisations, it is worthwhile comparing the relations between NPOs and public power in China and Germany by referring to the approach of corporatism. This will help to reveal the impact of different types of corporatism on state–society relations. More importantly, it may be helpful in answering the question of what kind of corporatism would be beneficial for Chinese society.

2 The Degree of Development and Function of NPOs in China and Germany

Both China and Germany recognise NPOs as organisations characterised by independence from government, being not for profit and self-governed, and by their formal structure. The most common legal forms of NPOs in Germany are registered associations, private law foundations, private limited corporations and cooperatives (Zimmer 2015).

There were 700,000 non-profit organisations in Germany in 2016. In the area of social service provision, NPOs are members of umbrella organisations—the Free Welfare Associations—that were founded in the early 1920s and still serve as lobbyists on behalf of the needy. Almost all German NPOs working in the area of social service provision are members of these six umbrellas, forming a tradition of sharing social service experience, exchanging professional information and jointly participating in social policies.

In China, there are three kinds of social organisations called membership organisations, social service organisations and foundations. By the end of 2016, there were 702,000 social organisations in China, including 336,000 membership organisations, 361,000 social service organisations and 5,559 foundations. Some similarities and differences can be found by comparing NPOs in China and Germany.

Similarities. First, the categories of social organisations, which are roughly divided into foundations, membership organisations and social service organisations in both countries, are basically similar.

Second, social organisations are in constant development. According to the available figures, there were 615,000 social organisations in Germany in 2011 and 700,000 in 2016. In China, the number rose from nearly 460,000 in 2011 to 702,000 in 2016. In about five years, that number in Germany increased by 85,000 and in China by 140,000 (Zhang and Huang 2012, 4–15).

Differences. First, the two countries have different densities of social organisations. From a purely quantitative perspective, Germany is one of the few countries in the world with one organisation per about 80 people on average. That is a higher density than most OECD countries like the United States, Britain and Japan. In China, with a total population of approx. 1.4 bn and 817,000 social organisations in 2018, there is one organisation per 1,708 people on average.

Second, Salamon has defined the attributes of social organisations (Salamon and Sokolowski 2007). However, in Germany, the most important denominator for NPOs is their tax-exempt status. And in China, the government has gradually adopted the concept of "social organisation" since 2004 to make it more flexible and inclusive, but the above-mentioned three kinds of organisations (membership organisations, social service organisations and foundations) are the only kinds of social organisations that can be registered (Ma 2015).

Third, there are differences in the role of social organisations in the two countries. According to a study by Germany's Civil Society in Numbers (ZiviZ) project, 649,708 NPOs provided 3.7 million jobs in 2016 as part of the third sector, or 9.9 % of the German workforce (Hohendanner et al. 2019). In 2007, their total spending was last calculated for 2007, amounting to €90 bn or 4.1 per cent of the country's GDP.[1]

According to the calculations and research by the team of the National Academy of Governance, the total expenditure of 700,000 registered social organisations in China in 2016 was about 87 billion euros, accounting for 0.86% of that year's GDP. In other words, the social service expenditure of 700,000 organisations in China in 2016 was less than that of 100,000 social organisations in Germany nine years earlier (MA et al. 2018).

Fourth, there are differences between the status of NPOs in the two countries. Germany has a long history of freedom of association. NPOs are

---

1 According to the Civil Society in Numbers (ZiviZ) report (Fritsch et al. 2011). This was a cooperation project between the German Federal Statistical Office, the Centre for Social Investment, the Bertelsmann Foundation, the Donors' association for the promotion of humanities and sciences in Germany and the Fritz Thyssen Foundation.

regarded as one of the five pillars of German democracy (Wang, Li, Huang 2006:28). After a decade of tortuous development since 1990, China's social organisations entered a stage of steady and rapid development from around 2000 (Xie and Ma 2015, 35–39). This new stage of development began because, on the one hand, the four-year period of the "Cleansing campaign of social organisations" (1997–2000) was over, and, on the other hand and even more importantly, along with the implementation of new regulations in 1999[2], a new form of social organisation called "private non-enterprise unit" (民办非企业单位)[3] was allowed to register. This accelerated the growth of social organisations in China, which reached the total number of 211,000 organisations in 2000[4]. However, their influence is relatively small because policy support is insufficient. In terms of private law foundations, there are at least 20,000 in Germany as of 2016. In the same year, there were fewer than 600 public law foundations in China (Bundesverband Deutscher Stiftungen 2017), and their supporting capacity needs to be strengthened. As far as membership organisations are concerned, the German government does not have a specific supervising agency, but they are under the supervision of the tax agencies in terms of their common weal-oriented/tax-exempt status. In Germany, NPOs are very important partners in public social service provision. They are paid for the services they provide but are not subsidised by the state. NPOs active in social welfare count economically for the most prominent part of the sector in Germany. Indeed, their share of total NPO employment amounts to ¾ (Zimmer et al. 2013).

Fifth, there are differences in NPO policy participation. Germany has a tradition of "joint decision-making" in which representatives of civil organisations generally participate in public decision-making consulting procedures (Scott 2011). Representatives of the major welfare associations are usually involved in the local council for children and youth. Here, NPOs are members of the policy formulating committee by law. Participation in other committees is not earmarked for NPOs (Wollmann and Schröter 2004, 276).

---

2 "Interim Regulations on Registration and Administration of Private Non-enterprise Unit " (Decree of the State Council of the PRC, No.251,1998.10.25); Interim Measures for the Registration of Private Non-enterprise Units" (Decree of the Ministry of Civil Affairs, PRC, No.18[1998], promulgated and implemented on 28 December 1999).

3 Recently renamed Social Service Organisations (社会服务机构).

4 Statistical Bulletin on the Development of Civil Affairs (1986–2009), China; Statistical Bulletin on Social Service Development (2010–2017), China.

Since 2002, China has advocated that social organisations participate in policy formulation. In 2013, NPO participation in democratic consultation was also proposed. NPOs had a great influence on the formulation of China's Charity Law in 2016. However, in practice, the country mainly focuses on NPOs' participation in social services. As for policy participation, no normative mechanism with an institutional guarantee exists.

Sixth, there are differences in NPO independence. The German government adheres to the principle of cooperation and maintains the appropriate boundary between it and civil organisations. Non-profit organisations are always autonomous legal entities. Even in the unique umbrella organisation of corporatism, government power does not interfere in their internal autonomy and basically does not get involved in their leadership, which becomes the premise of real cooperation between the two sides. However, most of the Chinese industry associations and chambers of commerce are separated from the original government departments along with the reforms. The leaders of associations are basically the officials from the power system. Since 2013, China has been striving to promote the separation of associations from public power. However, while progress has been made, other types of power have been implanted. The phenomenon called "political power absorbing society" (Kang, Han et al. 2007, 116–128) has affected the autonomy of social organisations in China.

3 Characteristics of the Relationship between Government and NPOs in China and Germany

The relationship between government and NPOs is mainly affected by at least seven aspects, namely types of corporatism, legal form, registration conditions, administration, tax policies, service cooperation and NPO governance. The differences in NPOs between China and Germany reflect the differences in political and social relations between the two countries to some extent.

3.1 Types of Corporatism in the Two Countries under Different Rationalities

According to Philippe C. Schmitter (1974), corporatism is an institutional arrangement about the model of interest representation. Compared with the freedom of association based on pluralism and the prevention of association based on regulationism, corporatism takes a middle path. Based on observation and research, Philippe C. Schmitter proposed the concepts of two subtypes, societal corporatism and state corporatism (Schmitter 1974, 103), and distinguishes them with indicators such as: number of associations, mode of restriction, mode of participation, representativeness, mode of approval, competitiveness and functional segmentation (Zhang 1998, 167).

Streeck and Kenworthy[5] (2005) go a little further and distinguish between "traditional corporatism", "state corporatism" and "liberal corporatism"/ "neocorporatism". Accordingly, *traditional corporatism* as a form of interest representation and state organisation existed in Germany in the 19th century and at the beginning of the 20th century. Based on Catholic social doctrine, political representation was organised on the basis of professional groups instead of liberal democratic institutions. Traditional corporatism was based on the constitutional principle of subsidiarity, according to which the state had to "refrain from activities that smaller social entities [could] perform by themselves and indeed [was] obliged to help them independently to govern their affairs" (Streeck and Kenworthy 2005, 443 f.). *State corporatism* is a state–society relationship in which the state uses "state-instituted corporate bodies as transmission belts of a governing party" (441). It is used as an instrument of state rule, in which society is compulsorily organised along the lines of industrial sectors and producer groups (444) and the state can intervene in the internal processes of the organisations (451). In contrast, "liberal corporatism" is, as Streeck and Kenworthy explain, a phenomenon observable in European post-war democracies, a form of "territorial rule, which now took place through parliamentary representation, shared the public space with social groups organised on a more voluntary basis and entitled to various forms of collective participation and self-government, provided they recognised the primacy of parliamentary democracy" (441). Finally, in *liberal corporatism/neocorporatism* "organised groups are tolerated by the constitutional order on condition that they limit themselves to lobbying the parliament and refrain from claiming rights, however circumscribed, to authoritative decision making" (441). In contrast to pluralism, in which organised interests are limited to the input side of the political process, in corporatism, "social interests participate not only in the making of binding decisions but also in their implementation" (448).

---

5 I would like to thank Matthias Stepan for pointing me towards Streeck and Kenworthy's discussion on the variants of corporatism.

Although the indicators for distinguishing "state corporatism" from "liberal corporatism" are not perfect, the subtype classification of corporatism is of great significance. According to these criteria, people can make judgements on the type of corporatism in a country, understand the nature of the relationship between public power and the civil rights of it, and gain an insight into the trend of its civil association. Combined with practical observation and literature research, we have supplemented Schmitter's as well as Streeck and Kenworthy's categorisations (Table 1).

Table 1: Comparison of the different influences of state corporatism and liberal corporatism on NPO

Indicator	State Corporatism	Liberal Corporatism
1. Policy environment	Discourage development of NPOs	No limitation of NPOs' development
2. Registration procedure	Harsh conditions and complex procedures	Simple conditions and procedures
3. Forms of establishment	Top-down	Bottom-up
4. Operator	Mainly the public sector	Mainly civilian
5. Origin of organisation's leader	Officially designated	Through democratic processes within NPO
6. Representation	By authority	Naturally formed
7. Government intervention in activities	Mainly by official arrangement	Mainly voluntary action
8. Sources of funds	Mainly from public funds	Multiple sources of funds
9. Competitiveness	Low competitiveness	High competitiveness
10. Business boundaries	Mainly by official arrangement	Mainly based on voluntary agreement
11. Motivation	Political order	Social order and freedom of association

Source: The Authors.

Germany looks back upon a long development of corporatism. In the area of welfare provision, Germany has formed a national network of NPOs providing social services with six umbrella organisations. They play an important role in coordinating relations with the government. Germany is undoubtedly an example of the practice of corporatism.

The Chinese government does not have a clear sense of corporatism, "institutionally speaking, corporatism seems to be very suitable for summarizing the relationship between the state and society in China." (Wu 2012, 180). A large number of GONGOs have revealed they have the characteristics of "limited number, singular, compulsory, non-competitive, hierarchically ordered" (Schmitter 1974, 103). This has aroused the enthusiasm of some scholars in China to use the theoretical tool of corporatism. They even think that corporatism is a better choice for the relationship between China's government and society.

3.2 Relationship Characteristics in Legal Form

Both countries have institutional arrangements and specific norms and values for NPOs. Also, their legal forms are different.

Germany is a civil law country. As the basic law, the German constitution recognises the will of citizens' groups and guarantees citizens' freedom of association. By guaranteeing freedom of association, German laws provide a broad scope for civic activities. The term 'association' refers to any group of natural or legal persons voluntarily united for a long period of time with a common purpose and able to express its meaning in an organised way. Beyond the freedom of association, there are many rules and legal stipulations regulating day-to-day procedures of NPOs in Germany.

China has a social organisation system based on the constitution, regulations and official policy documents. The Chinese constitution also stipulates that citizens shall have freedom of association, but in exercising their right of association they shall not impair the interests of the state, society or the collective and the lawful freedoms and rights of other citizens. In reality, China has set up a normative framework composed of three regulations, which stipulates the scope, nature, organisational mode, application procedures and supervision forms of three types of civil organisations (associations, social service agencies and foundations). In addition, for both internal and external reasons, authorities have formulated more than 60 documents since 1988 as the basis for the supervision of NPOs.

China's NPOs have not yet had a specific law; they have only been regulated by lower-level regulations and temporary documents. German legislation has a clear motivation for supporting civil society organisations. China usually encourages social service organisations while rather restricting advocacy organisations. The number of relevant legal texts in Germany is small, the content of provisions is concentrated and clear, and the implementation costs are low. There is a large number of regulatory texts on social organisations in China, with scattered contents and high implementation costs for all parties. The legal provisions on NPOs in Germany are stable. The contents of relevant regulatory documents in China are constantly changing, and the NPOs have only limited legal security.

3.3 Relationship Characteristics in Registration Conditions

It is one thing to recognise freedom of association through the constitution, but quite another to enforce it. Different registration conditions show the relationship between different public powers and private rights and also lead to different civil society growth results. Some registration requirements for the establishment of NPOs in Germany and China are similar. But there are several key rules that are different.

German law stipulates that seven or more people can go to the local court to register as an association. The registration fee is about 10 euros. Foundations come in a variety of forms. You can apply to the regional administration body (Regierungspräsidium) to register a foundation for 50,000 euros. A limited liability company costs approximately 25,000 euros. There is no specific provision for the supervision of contributors by law.

Registration requirements in China are stringent: NPO initiators must not only be vetted by the registration authority, but also by an additional so-called professional supervision unit.

To set up a nationwide membership organisation requires more than 10 initiators and at least RMB 100,000 Yuan for its registration. Setting up a local membership organisation requires more than 5 initiators and at least RMB 30,000 Yuan. Applicants first need permission from their employers, and then the agreement of an official to act as the organisation's supervisory unit. Only then can they start the registration process with the Ministry of Civil Affairs or its lower-level offices[6].

For the establishment of a foundation, a minimum of registered capital of RMB 2 million Yuan used to be required. The new draft regulations will raise the required amount of registered capital to at least RMB 8 million Yuan. The new regulations also stipulate that foundations have to register with registration organs at the provincial level or above[7].

The minimum registration fee for setting up a social service NPO (old term: private non-enterprise unit) is RMB 30,000 Yuan under current regulations. But in practice, government registration departments usually raise additional fees. In some places, the registration fee at the provincial level can reach RMB 500,000 Yuan or even 1 million Yuan. Most applications

---

6 Regulations on the Registration and Administration of Social Organizations (Draft for the Solicitation of Comments) Art. 17 (2). Ministry of Civil Affairs, PRC, 2018.).

7 Regulations on the Registration and Administration of Social Organizations (Draft for the Solicitation of Comments) Art. 23. Ministry of Civil Affairs, PRC, 2018.

also require approval from both the initiators' unit and the supervisory unit.

In conclusion, the registration conditions stipulated by German laws for the establishment of various NPOs are not easy but manageable. The registration requirements set by China's regulations are relatively stringent, which increases the leeway for political reviews of initiators. Unlike in Germany, in China, under the new draft rules, the registration authorities must decide whether to approve an application or not and inform the applicants within a maximum of 90 days[8].

3.4 Relationship Characteristics in Administration

The administration of NPOs in a certain country reflects the concept of public authority. Based on the status of the right to freedom of association, the degree of autonomy varies. Based on the political order, there will be different practices of control.

According to German law, the administration authorities are mainly responsible for the registration of civil associations. After registration is completed, control of an NPO is in the hands of the tax department. Local tax authorities require such organisations to have regular financial reports. The financial department conducts financial inspections every three years to ensure that the organisation complies with the non-profit principles stipulated in its articles of association. But all in all, the authorities should not interfere too much, and should not even adopt the so-called mode of "supervision" as practised in China[9]. In reality, there is no supervision department specially set up for civil society organisations in Germany. There are no registration procedures other than by the local courts and the regional governments. There are no annual inspections of NPOs, except regular checks by the tax authorities. And there is no disclosure of NPOs' in-

---

8 Regulations on the Registration and Administration of Social Organizations (Draft for the Solicitation of Comments) Art. 20, 26, 31. Ministry of Civil Affairs, PRC, 2018.

9 I.e. the registration and administration authority is responsible for investigating and punishing suspected illegal acts by NPOs, including on-site inspection, access to relevant files and enquiring about financial accounts. The supervisory unit is responsible for examining NPOs' annual reports and assisting in the investigation of suspected illegal acts. The Communist Party's working organs are responsible for conducting political reviews of the leaders of NPOs (Regulations on the Registration and Administration of Social Organizations (Draft for the Solicitation of Comments) Article 66, 67, 68. Ministry of Civil Affairs, PRC, 2018).

formation required by regulations. Only extremist groups and terrorist groups will be punished by law. And also, if the activities of the association conflict with the constitution and criminal law, as well as with international goodwill and national unity, the association's legal person status will be terminated by judicial procedures. But so far this has been rare.

Due to political order concerns, China has a relatively large number of NPO regulations. Supervision includes: qualification of sponsors, examination of establishment conditions, examination of political obligations, audit of financial accounts, supervision of activities, disclosure of internal information, disposition of violations, etc. A pluralistic surveillance and control network has been formed around the NPOs. Among them, the main regulators are registration authorities and competent departments. Assisting regulators include the government's diplomatic, public security, pricing, fiscal, social security, taxation, auditing and financial authorities. The local organs of the party are mainly responsible for political supervision.

It can be seen that there is an equal relationship between the German government and NPOs. The government does not advocate administrative intervention in civil society but pursues the principles of autonomy and self-discipline. The supervision and control of NPOs is stricter in China. Not only do regulators involve multiple departments of the party and government, but their regulatory power is also strong. However, recently China emphasised the principle of reciprocity of power and obligations and began to implement internal information disclosure measures for NPOs.

3.5 Relationship Characteristics in Tax Policies

German law grants organisations tax exemption based on the nature and intent of their activities. Only those organisations that work in the public interest are eligible for tax-exempt status. This qualification needs to be examined and approved by the financial authority. Tax-exempt status translates into the situation that the organisation need not to pay corporate tax. It does not mean that any activity by the NPO which generates income is tax exempt (Strachwitz 2006).

The Chinese tax law stipulates that the income of institutions engaged in basic welfare services, medical services, educational services, agricultural technology training, religious sites and public cultural services is exempt from VAT (tax rate 3%). An NPO's income from donations, government subsidies and membership dues, and deposit interest from tax-free income are exempt from income tax (tax rate 25%). The premise is that the organisation's tax-exempt status must be recognised by the tax authorities. Other exemptions, such as land occupation tax, property tax, and vehicle and ship tax, are currently available only to state-run social organisations, but not to civil NPOs (Ma 2014, 163).

To sum up, both countries may be cautious with regard to tax exemption due to worries about affecting market fairness and tax sources. However, the German government takes a more liberal stance towards tax exemption than the Chinese. The Chinese government exempts VAT for specific public services, while limiting the exemption of income tax from operating income, which especially puts pressure on the maintenance and appreciation of funds. What's more, the Chinese government also needs to change the inequality between GONGOs[10] and NPOs in its tax exemption policy.

3.6 Relationship Characteristics in Service Cooperation

There is a global trend towards cooperation between government and NPOs in the provision of public services. Both the Chinese and German governments have basically the same understanding of the value of cooperation, that is, to promote social participation in public welfare, stimulate citizens' sense of responsibility and expand the resources of public services. Only, in practice, the two countries differ in degree and fairness in this respect.

Germany has a long history of NPOs providing social welfare services. The relationship between the government and NPOs is not only a form of equal cooperation, but the systematic, professional and comprehensive welfare services of NPOs also make the government dependent on it. In the service system, which is mainly composed of non-profit organisations, commercial organisations and local governments, NPOs play a leading role in most welfare services, providing more than 70% of the total services (Zimmer et al. 2013). The services of business organisations rank second. Although German local governments are also involved in providing some public services, they are mainly responsible for regulation and policies. NPOs' social service funds have multiple sources, such as donations, foundation grants, membership fees and social insurance payments. If the

---

10 Government-operated NGOs with Chinese characteristics in terms of organisation and funding from the government. Their staff have the status of civil servants; their leaders are appointed by the government and they enjoy certain privileges.

funds regulated by the government, such as service remuneration, which is covered by social and health insurance, are characterised as "public funds", government regulated financing of NPOs amounts to ⅔ of the total NPO revenue (Zimmer et al. 2007).

The Chinese government established cooperative relations with social organisations through public services in Shanghai in 1995. Over the past 20 years, this cooperative relationship has been gradually strengthened. In 2013, the central government of China implemented the policy of 'the government purchasing services from social forces', which has been widely implemented by local governments through the purchase of services and cooperation with social organisations. The services of social organisations cover poverty relief, support for vulnerable groups, community development, environmental protection and public culture, etc. Like the German government's policy, the service purchase mechanism gradually moves towards competitive bidding. The funding structure of social organisations is diversified. Depending on the sampling calculation, the total service expenditure of China's registered NPOs in 2016 was about RMB 672 billion Yuan (about 87 billion euros) (Ma et al. 2018). About half of that money comes from public funds. The Chinese government has gradually established an institutionalised system in its service cooperation with social organisations.

The cooperation between the German government and NPOs is characterised by a long history. NPOs have certain policy discourse rights in the field of welfare services. Although the time of cooperation between the government and NPOs in China is only about 20 years, with recent years having witnessed rapid development and the transparency of public financial funds gradually improving. However, due to a large number of GONGOs in China, sometimes the fairness of cooperation becomes a challenge. Some projects contracts are directly awarded to those GONGOs (the so-called "insiders") without tendering in procedure. It is common, too, for some local governments to entrust projects and funds to those political mass organisations ("insiders") as hubs, and then to subcontract to other NPOs (the so-called "outsiders"). This practice might significantly undermine NPOs' independence.

3.7 Relationship Characteristics in NPO Governance

The core of NPO governance is autonomy and democracy. One of the key indicators of governance is how the main leaders of an organisation are selected. This not only affects the degree of its independence but also fundamentally determines the nature of the relationship between the public authorities and NPOs.

German NPOs mainly embody the characteristics of autonomy. After social organisations have registered, the federal, regional and local governments generally do not interfere in them. Organisations basically have no government-appointed officials as leaders, and few organisations are established under the control of the German government. Even the public finance-supported party foundations and the foundations based on public law are run by an elected council. They employ professional managers and have a mechanism of checks and balances in accordance with the articles of association to ensure the autonomy of NPOs.

At this point, power has an important influence in the internal management of China's NPOs. Although autonomy and democracy are written in the charters of all organisations, the shadow of power behind social organisations can be seen everywhere in practice. For example, there are fifteen extremely large social organisations that are exempt from registration, and their organisation network covers the whole country (e.g. the China Law Society, the China Writers' Association, the All-China Journalists' Association and the China Vocational Education Association). There are more than 70,000 business associations accounting for one fifth of the total number of national associations mainly run by public departments. Some organisations cannot decide on their own leaders. Some are initiated by retired government officials. In addition, the work of the party and with the nature of public power has also become an important factor that affects NPOs (Ma 2014).

4 *The Rationality behind the Relationship between Government and Social Organisations*

There is no doubt that the development and role of NPOs in China and Germany are significantly different. In this section, we discuss further what affects the relationships between government and NPOs. The government plays a major role in them. Whether it is based on usefulness, respect or both in order to build their relationship with civil organisations, it is the choice of the powerful participant in the relationship. Here, "instrumental rationality" and "value rationality" are introduced to analyse the underlying consciousness of their behaviour, and then analyse the direction of freedom of association affected by the domination of their respective consciousness.

Max Weber introduced the concepts of "instrumental rationality" and "value rationality". He believed that instrumental rationality is "the subjective will and choices of action for achieving goals through the conditions that can be utilized or the means available" (Weber 1997:56). That is to say, in order to achieve a certain purpose, people will choose the mode of action that they think is most effective. Therefore, those who prefer instrumental rationality do not care about the good or evil of the action but are only concerned whether the action is effective in regard to the purpose. Instrumental rationality often treats external conditions (including people, methods, environmental conditions) as tools or barriers to achieving their goals.

Value rationality, by contrast, "is a conscious and unconditional belief in the intrinsic value of a particular action, regardless of whether the outcome of that action is successful or not" (Weber 1997:56). That is to say, behaviour subjectively makes the action selected "good" regardless of any other purpose. Those who are inclined to value rationality only care about or mainly care about the self-value of the action, and do not calculate the instrumental effect of the action.

From the perspective of instrumental rationality and value rationality, the way in which the two governments deal with NPOs can hardly produce an absolute result for either or both. The two governments display neither pure instrumental rationality nor purely value rationality. However, it can be seen that they show significant differences in value rationality under a certain degree of instrumental rationality. Both governments apply instrumental rationality in that they recognise that NPOs are an important social service force.

The German government's position is that: "non-profit organizations can help the government to reduce the burden of social affairs and have a higher input-output ratio than the government to provide social welfare services. Because first, giving social welfare services to non-profit organisations can make citizens more socially responsible and motivate them. Second, on the basis of government funding, non-profit organisations can raise funds from society and even invest their own funds, which produces a multiplier effect of funds. Third, non-profit organisations can pool human resources in the society, attract more volunteers to participate in public welfare projects, and greatly reduce service costs" (Li 2008).

The position of the Chinese government is that "reforming the management system of social organisations and promoting the healthy and orderly development of social organisations are conducive to clarifying the boundaries between the government, the market and society and improving the socialist market economic system. It is conducive to improving the mode of public services supply as well as strengthening and innovating governance. It is conducive to stimulating social vitality and consolidating and expanding the ruling foundation of the party".[11]

While treating NPOs as service partners, the German government demonstrates more value rationality than instrumental rationality, that is, by recognising and affirming the natural rights and values of NPOs. The legal status of German NPOs comes from the spirit of the constitution: The state cannot be a top-down will tool. The state should guarantee that individuals can participate in state affairs from the bottom up. The state should cooperate with society and safeguard the basic rights of citizens. In line with this, article 20 of the German constitution stipulates—among other things—that all the power of the state comes from the people. The power of the state shall be exercised by the people by election and referenda, and by separate legislative, executive and judicial powers. State power is determined by citizens through voting and is exercised by separate legislative, executive and judicial power. Article 9 stipulates that all Germans have the right to associate. The purpose or activities of associations shall be prohibited if they contravene the criminal law or violate the constitutional order or international understanding. The right to protect and promote labour and economic conditions should be guaranteed to anyone and any profession. Any agreement that restricts or obstructs this right is void and the measures taken for this purpose are illegal[12]. Therefore, both the government's utilitarian intentions and respect for the rights of civil organisations are involved in the cooperation between the German government and NPOs. The latter as value rationality is at least not weaker than the former as instrumental rationality.

The Chinese Constitution also provides that "all power of the state belongs to the people". Article 35 also clarifies that "citizens of the People's Republic of China have freedom of speech, publication, assembly, association, procession, and demonstration". This is consistent with the basic spirit of freedom of association in the international community. What is different from Germany is that the freedom of association in the Chinese Constitution is not fully implemented. And it is also not possible to claim one's right at a national constitutional court in China. The institutional

---

11 General Office of the State Council, 2016: Guidelines on Reform of the Social Organization System to Promote healthy and orderly development of social organizations. Online: http://www.gov.cn/xinwen/2016-08/22/content_5101379.htm, accessed on 22 March 2020.

12 German Constitution in Chinese version. https://www.douban.com/group/topic/61786897/ .

environment for the growth of Chinese civil society is mainly composed of the constitution, common law, administrative regulations, party policies and other informal rules, which form an institutional network that affects the development of civil society. In the 1980s, China once had the intention to encourage freedom of association. The Ministry of Civil Affairs drafted the Association Law in 1987, but it was not adopted in the end. The subsequent political wave led the government to form a double or even triple registration method for NPOs. The "Regulations on the Registration and Administration of Social Organizations (Draft for the Solicitation of Comments)" (2018) continue to show the government's intention of controlling associations. Compared with the enthusiasm of the Chinese government for purchasing social organisation services since 2012, it is more about the instrumental consideration of fulfilling its functions. Therefore, it can be said that the Chinese government applies more instrumental rationality than value rationality in dealing with civil society organisations.

Although we can find features of different forms of corporatism in China and Germany, it is worth checking the relationships between NPOs and government in more detail. In Table 2, we compare the actual characteristics of the corporatism relations in the two countries according to the indicators listed in Table 1.

Table 2: Summary of Characteristics of Chinese and German Corporatism

Indicator	China	Germany
1. Policy environment	Differential treatment, **restricting development**	*No limitation of NPO development,* all organisations equally treated.
2. Registration procedure	**Conditions for setting up civil NPOs are stringent; at least three thresholds needed to pass the approval process; strict supervision.**	*Few conditions for establishing NPOs;* the approval procedure and the prohibition conditions are rather simple; supervision only over tax-exempt NPOs.
3. Forms of establishment	15 large organisations without registration requirement and with nationwide networks; nearly one-third of public fundraising foundations, nearly one-fifth of associations, and one-third of social service organisations are formed from the **top down**, while the rest is established bottom-up.	Almost all NPOs are formed *bottom-up*, and very few public law foundations are funded by federal or federal state governments.

Indicator	China	Germany
4. Operator	GONGOs are usually run by the public sector; Party organisations in NPOs are involved in important decisions.	Almost all civil organisations *have no affiliation relations with government*, and only a few public law foundations have a government background.
5. Origin of the organisation's leader	Leaders at all levels of the 15 large organisations without registration requirement and with nationwide networks, and the leaders of nearly one-third of the public fundraising foundations, nearly one-fifth of the associations' leaders, as well as government-established social service agencies, **are basically determined by government**; the leaders of civil NPOs are generated internally.	The leaders of almost all civil society organisations are *generated by internal election mechanisms*.
6. Representation	Without an absolute representative mechanism; GONGOs and those with an official background have more opportunities than NPOs to enter People's Congresses and Political Consultation meetings.	There is no exclusive representation mechanism, but some NPOs *have representatives in policy committees*.
7. Government intervention in activities	The activities of GONGOs and those with a power background are usually more affected by the government, while NPOs are passive.	Activities of all organisations are *self-directed*, including the Public Law Foundations
8. Sources of funds	**Mainly from public funds**; the 15 large organisations without registration requirement and with nationwide networks are fully funded by the government; some GONGOs and those with an official background have advantages in obtaining public funds; powerful industrial and commercial associations self-funded; civil NPOs by competition.	Civil NPOs depending on *multiple funds*, 60 per cent of welfare NPOs' income comes from government funding in a competitive bidding process; very few public law foundations supported mainly by government funding; other organisations mainly by raising funds themselves.
9. Competitiveness	Low competition for the GONGOs and high competition for civil organisations.	*High competition* for almost all NPOs.

Indicator	China	Germany
10. Business boundaries	Large-scale network organisations such as industry associations and chambers of commerce with official backgrounds are basically unique and **restrict the establishment of similar organisations.**	Mainly based on *voluntary agreement*; associations are mainly based on professional and voluntary agreements, and there is no government will.
11. Motivation	There are also political order considerations and economic considerations, but **political factors are prominent.**	There are both social order and welfare service considerations, as well as *freedom of association rights.*

Compilated by the authors. Bold sections indicate state corporatism; itallics indicate liberal corporatism.

Thus, this paper can draw some conclusions on the characteristics of the relationship between government and society and the phenomenon of social organisations.

Table 2 shows that, on the Chinese side, 3 of the 11 indicators are highly consistent with the characteristics of state corporatism, such as the limitation of the number of associations, the severity and complexity of control, and political motivation in the development of NPOs. 5 of the 11 indicators are more or less in line with the characteristics of state corporatism, such as the origin of the organisations' leaders, the forms of establishment, the operator, sources of funds and professional field division. As for the other indicators, such as representation, government intervention in activities and competitiveness, the privileged characteristics of China's GONGOs stand in sharp contrast to those of NPOs and, in fact, they also correspond with state corporatism to a certain degree.

On the German side, at least 9 of the 11 indicators are highly consistent with the characteristics of liberal corporatism, such as: the unlimited number of associations, simple and convenient registration, the motivation for free association, bottom-up organisation, operation by autonomous actors, the leaders being self-generated, activities being autonomous from state intervention, the funding resources being manifold and professional field division being by voluntary agreements. The remaining two items, representativeness and competitiveness, also correspond more with liberal corporatism.

Therefore, it can be argued that the relationship between the government and social organisations, and also the direction of association development in China, has a tendency towards state corporatism between corporatism and regulationism, which is mainly implied by *instrumental* rationality. Germany, on the other hand, has a tendency towards liberal corporatism, between corporatism and pluralism, which implies *value* rationality. Under the different rationalities, the two countries have formed very different types of corporatism, which in turn generate different relationships with their respective characteristics and affect the trend of their civil society and their social status.

5 Conclusion

The above analysis helps deepen the following understandings: First, the relationship between the government and social organisations and the development of associations in both countries are obviously characterised by corporatism, but they are quite different from each other.

Secondly, corporatism gets its true meaning in its subtypes. In real life, it is either state corporatism or liberal corporatism.

Third, the formation of liberal corporatist relations between the state and society is inseparable from the normal market economy, mature civil society, and a certain foundation of liberal democracy and the rule of law. Only with these three conditions can state corporatism be prevented from distorting the development of civil society, weakening civil rights such as free association, and harming the benign cooperation between the government and civil organisations.

References

Bundesverband Deutscher Stiftungen (ed.) (2017). *Zahlen, Daten, Fakten zum deutschen Stiftungswesen.* Berlin: Bundesverband Deutscher Stiftungen.

Chen, Feng (2003). "Between the State and Labor: The Conflict of Chinese Trade Unions' Dual Institutional Identity." *The China Quarterly*, 176, 1006–1028.

Chen, Jiajian (2010). "Corporatism and Contemporary Chinese Society", *Sociological Research*, 2010, No. 2, 30–43.

Clark, Simon (2005). "Post socialist Trade Unions: China and Russia." *Industrial Relations Journal*, 36.

Cui, Kaiyun (2017). "Corporate Governance Model in the Field of Social Services in Germany", *Social Scientist*, 3.

Deng Guosheng (2001). "Preliminary Analysis of the Questionnaire Survey of Chinese NGOs". *Chinese NGO Research.*

Fan, Minglin (2010). "The Interaction between NGOs and Government", *Sociological Research*, 3, 159–176.

Fritsch, Sigrid et al. 2011, *Abschlussbericht Modul 1, ZiviZ Zivilgesellschaft in Zahlen*, April 2011. Online available at http://ziviz.info/sites/ziv/files/zivilgesellschaft_in_zahlen_abschlussbericht_modul_1.pdf, (last access: 29 March 2020).

Gu, Xin and Xu Wang 2005 "From Nationalism to Corporatism: the Evolution of the Relationship between the State and Professional Groups in China's Market Transition", *Sociological Research*, 2, 155–117.

Henriksen, Lars Skov and Steven Rathgeb Smith, Annette Zimmer (2012). "At the Eve of Convergence? Transformation of Social Service Provision in Denmark, Germany, and the United States", *Voluntas*, 23:2, 458–501.

Hohendanner, Christian and Jana Priemer, Boris Rump, Wolfgang Schmitt (2019) "Zivilgesellschaft als Arbeitsmarkt." In Holger Krimmer (ed.): *Datenreport Zivilgesellschaft*. Wiesbaden: Springer VS, 93–112.

Howell, Jude (2003). "Trade Unionism in China: Sinking or Swimming", *Journal of Communist Studies and Transition Politics*, 19:1.

Kang, Xiaoguang et al. (2007) "Administrative Absorption Society – a Study on the Relationship between State and Society in Mainland China", *Social Science in China*, 2, 116–128.

Li, Yong (2008). *German Non-Profit Organization Management Report*. Online available at: http://www.interhoo.com/content/4274.aspx.

Ma, Qingyu et al. (2018). *Measurement Report for Economic Scale of Registered Social Organizations in China*, Beijing.

Ma, Qingyu (2015). *Development strategy of social organizations in China*. Beijing: Social Sciences Academic Press.

Ma Qingyu (2014a) "Promoting the Reform of Government-run Social Organizations", *Vision of Contemporary Social Science*, 11.

Ma Qingyu (2014b). *NPOs in the Era of Governance in China*, Beijing: China National Academy of Governance Press.

Pang, Jinyou (2008). "Theoretical Debate on the Relationship Model between the State and Society in the Process of Globalization", *Teaching and Research*, 2, 655–671.

Pearson, Margaret M. (1994). "The Janus Face of Business Associations in China: Socialist Corporatism in Foreign Enterprises", *The Australian Journal of Chinese Affairs*, 31.

Salamon, Lester M. and S. Wojciech Sokolowski (2007). *Global Civil Society: Dimension of the Non-Profit Sector*, Vol. 2, (English edition: Kumarian Press 2004), Chinese edition, Beijing University Press.

Salamon, Lester M. (1994). "The Rise of the Nonprofit Sector," *Foreign Affairs*, 74:3.

Scott, Richard W. (2011). *Organizational Theory: Rational, Natural and Open Systems*, Beijing: Renmin University of China Press.

Wang, Ming and Yong Li, Haoming Huang (2006). *German Non-profit Organizations*, Beijing: Tsinghua University Press.

Schmitter, Phillippe C. (1974). "Still the Century of Corporatism?" *The Review of Politics*, 36:1, 85–131.

Strachwitz, Rupert Graf (2006). "German associations and foundations – service providers or civil society subjects?" In Ami Gutman et al. *Associations: Theory and Practice*, Beijing: Sanlian Bookstore.

Streeck, Wolfgang and Lane Kenworthy (2005). "Theories and practices of neocorporatism." In Thomas Janoski, Robert R. Alford, Alexander M. Hicks and M. A. Schwartz (eds.), The Handbook of Political Sociology: States, Civil Societies, and Globalization. Cambridge: Cambridge University Press, 441–460.

Wang, Xiangmin (2008). "Worker maturity and Societal Corporatism: a Study on the Transformation of Trade Unions in China", *Economic and Social System Comparison*.

Weber, Max (1997). *Economy and Society*, vol. 1, Trans. by Lin Rongyuan, Beijing: Commercial Press.

Wollmann, Hellmut and Eckhard Schröter (eds.) (2004). *Comparing the British–German Public Sector Reform*, Beijing: Peking University Press.

Wu, Jianping (2012). "Understanding Corporatism", *Sociology Research*, 1.

Xie, Ju and Qingyu Ma (2015). "A Review of the Development of Social Organizations in China". *Journal of Yunnan Academy of Governance*, 1, 35–39.

Zhang, Jing (1998) *Corporatism*, Beijing: China Social Science Press.

Zhang, Wangcheng and Haoming Huang (2012) "German Non-profit Organizations: Status, Characteristics and Development Trend", *German Research*, 27:2, 4–15.

Zimmer, Annette (1999). "Corporatism Revisited – The Legacy of History and the German Nonprofit-Sector", *Voluntas*, 10:1, 37–49.

Zimmer, Annette (2015). "Germany´s Nonprofit Organizations. Continuity and Change", *Sociologia e Politiche Sociali*, 18:3, 9–26.

Zimmer, Annette and Eckhard Priller (2007) *Gemeinnützige Organisationen im gesellschaftlichen Wandel. Ergebnisse der Dritte-Sektor-Forschung.* Wiesbaden: Springer VS Verlag.

Zimmer, Annette and Eckhard Priller, Helmut Anheier (2013). "Der Nonprofit-Sektor in Deutschland." In Ruth Simsa, Michael Meyer, Christoph Badelt, Christoph (eds.): *Handbuch der Nonprofit-Organisation*. 5th edition, Stuttgart: Schäffer-Poeschel, 15–36.

Conclusion

Beth Lovelady and Anja Ketels

The LoGoSO project was an opportunity to compare two very different countries where local municipalities share a similar responsibility, providing services for large, newly arrived migrant populations. Over a period of three years, the Chinese and German research teams looked at public administration traditions and trends in China and Germany, at the challenges in public service provision resulting from large-scale migration to the four sample cities (Berlin, Cologne, Guangzhou, Hangzhou), as well as at projects to address these challenges that were cooperative efforts between local governments and NPOs. The results of the observations are captured in nineteen working papers and nineteen case study reports.[1] The contributions in this book compile and analyse the results that were assembled over the course of the research project and reflect on different aspects of the research interests in China and Germany, such as models of public administration, state–society relations, local government and NPO responses to the challenges of migration, as well as cooperation models and characteristics of the cooperation between local governments and NPOs. This conclusion provides a round-up of the overall results of the LoGoSO project. It begins by outlining the results regarding state–society relations from a public administration perspective. Subsequently, it summarises the local government responses to the challenges of migration and the role of NPOs, followed by a review of the results regarding the modes of cooperation between local governments and NPOs, including the cooperation models and the factors that influence them. A summary of the results with regard to the differences and similarities between China and Germany concludes this chapter.

---

1 Most of the working papers and case study reports are available in the LoGoSO Research Papers publication series in the repository of Freie Universität Berlin: https://refubium.fu-berlin.de/handle/fub188/17676?locale-attribute=de.

State–Society Relations in Transformation: from Corporatism towards Neoliberalism

Even while China and Germany have divergent cultures, economies and political systems, they are both in the midst of a post-corporatist era of government and NPO cooperation that is highly influenced by principles of New Public Management[2]. The nature of state–society relations in Germany and China is central to how municipalities have responded to the steep challenges presented by serving large migrant populations.

As the authors in this book have highlighted, the transition from a corporatist to a more neoliberal system occurred at separate times and stemmed from different political systems in each country. Germany's transformation away from corporatism began at the start of 1990s and China's after the turn of the century. Ma, Xie and Li explain that Germany is a civil law country with a constitution that guarantees freedom of association, while China has a complex system for social organisations, based on the constitution, regulations and official policy documents, which includes freedom of association, albeit a more restricted version. In practice, this means that the processes and regulations around forming and managing associations in Germany are transparent, clear and relatively inexpensive, while in China barriers to entry are high and regulations are constantly changing. These obstacles, along with the fact that Germany has a much longer history of free association, while rapid development of Chinese NGOs didn't occur until the 2000s, have resulted in the establishment of significantly more NPOs per person in Germany than China (80:1 vs. 1714:1 in 2018).

Ma et al. also highlight the important differences in the type of corporatism in each country. In China, there is a form of state corporatism that leans towards regulationism and authoritarianism on a scale of freedom versus prevention of association. Whereas in Germany, the form is closer to liberal corporatism, on the side of freedom and pluralism. In line with this, Germany has a history of involving NPOs in policy processes, while in China there are no established mechanisms for policy participation. Levy and Ketels explain that China's version of corporatism was very pronounced in the 1980s and 1990s, when most civil organisations in China were "government-organised non-governmental organisations" (GONGOs), i.e. founded by the state or the Communist Party. The GONGOs

---

2 See Zimmer and Grabbe in this volume for more details on New Public Management.

kept in close alignment with the priorities of the party state and served as bridges between the state and society. Zimmer and Grabbe highlight that German corporatism was shaped around government cooperation with the independently established Welfare Associations that enjoyed a privileged position within Germany's welfare system up until the 1990s. While the political contexts and forms of corporatism differ in each country, the Lo-GoSO project has illuminated similarities in the way government and NPO cooperation has evolved over time, specifically in response to challenges posed by migrant integration.

Historically, Germany and China share a similar trajectory in the growth of charitable endeavours in the early 19th century and the subsequent abolition of private charitable institutions during the Nazi regime and at the start of the People's Republic of China (Gluns, 2018; Ketels, 2019). Post WWII, Germany saw the reestablishment of these historical charitable institutions, which became the core of the corporatist structure of Welfare Associations. However, by the 1990s, the Welfare Associations were perceived as quasi-governmental organisations that were out of touch with the needs of society, which, combined with the push towards neoliberal/New Public Management practices that favoured competition, led to the Welfare Associations losing their privileged position (Zimmer, 1999). As Zimmer and Grabbe explain, Germany's corporatism then shifted to a more pluralist system, in which Welfare Associations were forced to compete with other NPOs and for-profit enterprises to provide social welfare services.

The resurgence of China's third sector began in the 1980s following the introduction of the Reform and Opening Policies (Simon 2013). The 1990s were still characterised by strict incorporation of NPOs into state structures and only a slow diversification of the sector. Starting in 2000, the state gradually became more accepting of institutional plurality and rapid development of privately initiated organisations began. As Ma et al. noted, like Germany, China moved away from a strict corporatist system and incorporated New Public Management practices into the coordination of public services. Today, not least because of the currently restricting political environment, many Chinese NPOs that are involved in public services are privately organised and abstain from interest representation between the state and society for good reasons.

The case studies in the LoGoSO project show that both in Germany and China the state involves NPOs in service provision for migrants. However, the relationship types between the two are more diverse than either state corporatism or liberal corporatism would suggest. The cooperation in our cases show considerations of efficiency, reduction of costs and networks rather than interest representation and can thereby be better located in the recently evolved neoliberal context in both countries.

While the Welfare Associations are less privileged than before in Germany and while GONGOs have greatly reduced positions in the local welfare systems of China, they both still sometimes benefit from their previous status. In Germany, the Welfare Associations still have significant influence over the provision of social services. In China, GONGOs in some areas are still considered the preferred providers and are able to circumvent competitive bidding processes and have sometimes simplified registration and supervision conditions.

Challenges Posed by Migration: Local Government Responses

It is this legacy of a corporatist structure, combined with the more pluralist and neoliberal forms of government and NPO cooperation, that define local-level responses to large migrant populations. In both countries, the responsibility for integration falls heavily upon municipalities (Ketels, 2019). As Levy and Ketels state, while the nature of these migrant populations is very different, the challenges faced by local administrations to provide responsive social services in the absence of adequate resources and expertise are very similar. However, efforts in China are more focused on the creation and implementation of concepts which permit the integration of migrants into the social security system, while in Germany, the primary need is the development of the service provision infrastructure, which ultimately helps to fully integrate migrants into the local society (Ketels, 2019).

In Germany, even with its long history of hosting guest workers and asylum seekers, municipalities were not prepared to accommodate the unprecedented number of migrants arriving from war-torn countries, such as Syria, Iran and Afghanistan, in 2015 and 2016. In China, the economic development started by the Reform and Opening Policies of the 1980s led to mass migration of people from poor rural areas to wealthy cities, where restrictive household registration policies left these floating populations without access to local social service systems. The nineteen LoGoSO case studies look closely at how four cities in Germany and China, Berlin, Cologne, Guangzhou, and Hangzhou, responded to these integration challenges in the areas of employment, social assistance, vulnerable groups and education.

The arrival of so many migrants in 2015 and 2016 did not drastically change local public administration in Cologne and Berlin. Both cities have a long history of migration and share the value of diversity as a strength.

Further, local policy is focused on early integration strategies in recognition of the fact that migrants are likely to remain in the cities for a long time (Gluns, 2018; Grabbe, 2018). Even before the dramatic increase in migrant populations in 2015, each city provided integration services above and beyond what is required by national law and had consultative mechanisms to directly include migrants in policy processes.

In response to the arrival of so many migrants in Berlin, the internal governance structure was slightly reorganised to allow for improved coordination of migrant services (Gluns, 2018). In Cologne, the public administration structure was maintained; however, additional staff positions were added to focus directly on refugee issues (Grabbe, 2018).

Guangzhou and Hangzhou have been greatly impacted by the rapid economic development and urbanisation process in China since the 1980s. In the past three decades, they have become immigrant cities with a high percentage of migrant workers, who in some areas already outnumber the local population (Ketels 2019). The public administration authorities in the cities had no experience with migration and were not prepared to integrate migrating populations into the social security system. When realising the difficulties arising from a lack of social security, the municipalities gradually developed policies and mechanisms to deal with these challenges. Guangzhou is considered a national pioneer city regarding urbanisation and the management of migrant workers in the city having started initial migrant support policies in the mid-2000s. Hangzhou followed suit with its own local policies in 2012. However, these initial regulations did not address the restrictive household registration system (hukou), which remained the main obstacle to lasting integration. Since 2014, a points-based residence permit[3] has been promoted at the national level, which has only been beneficial to migrants who were already successfully settled in the city (Ketels 2019). The city administration authorities still struggle to integrate the large numbers of migrants who are not eligible to apply for household registration into the social security system, and the development of selective measures to manage the service provision for migrants is an ongoing process (Ketels 2019).

---

3 The points-based residence permit is a system that allows migrants to accumulate points based on certain qualifications in order for them to apply for household registration (hukou) at their place of residency. The rules for the accumulation of points are specified in the "Points-Based Residence Permit Index" and include qualifications such as duration of residency, professional qualification or tax payments made to the municipality.

Challenges Posed by Migration: The Role of NPOs

The responsibility for overall management of integration services rests with the main municipal administration agencies in all four of the Lo-GoSO sample cities. All of these main municipal administration bodies share this responsibility with district-level administration authorities and coordinate service provision with several agencies in different policy areas (Ketels, 2019). From an external public administration perspective, each city's administration further coordinates service provision with NPOs. The LoGoSO case studies highlight that migrant integration services in these four cities rely heavily upon NPOs. These NPOs bring expertise, connections to the migrant communities, and additional resources in the form of private funding and volunteers to public integration efforts. As noted by Levy and Ketels, this study looked at local government and NPO cooperation from both a top-down and a bottom-up perspective. From the top-down point of view, government cooperation with NPOs is examined within the framework of third-party government. From the bottom-up perspective, network governance provides the lens for looking at NPOs who cooperate with the government.

In Germany, elements of third-party government are embodied in municipal integration policy. In Cologne, the guiding policy on integration efforts, the "Concept to Strengthen Integrative Urban Society" (Konzept zur Stärkung der Integrativen Stadtgesellschaft), passed in 2013, was both developed in cooperation with NPOs and deems government and NPO cooperation necessary to success (Grabbe, 2018). In Berlin, the "Master Plan for Integration and Security" (Masterplan Integration und Sicherheit) outlines the importance of NPOs in migrant service provision (Gluns 2018).

In China, government purchasing of services is the predominant system with which to outsource service provision from the government to NPOs. Since the mid-2000s a series of policies starting with the "Government Procurement Law of the People's Republic of China" from 2002 has promoted the systematic involvement of NPOs in service provision and regulated the institutionalisation of government–NPO cooperation.

Local Government–NPO Cooperation: Models of Cooperation

In the analysis offered by Levy and Ketels, we see that in the majority of the Chinese and German cases, in which local governments are outsourcing migrant integration services to NPOs, this is the central form of cooperative activities. These local governments resort to outsourcing to harness

NPO expertise, provide public services and fulfil state and national requirements. In the case of China, the outsourcing is also used to maintain social stability by having NPOs provide services that address social unrest and by maintaining a certain level of control over these NPOs to ensure that their work is aligned with government objectives. In Germany, outsourcing is complementary and local government provides services in all the relevant policy areas, but those services are heavily supplemented by the work of NPOs. In China, migrant services in all four policy areas are completely outsourced to NPOs; in each area, local government either cannot or will not provide the services needed.

The case studies clearly show that there was a willingness to cooperate on both sides. From the bottom-up perspective, NPOs in both countries were engaged in migrant integration efforts both inside and outside of cooperative efforts with local government and they approached this work from a network governance perspective. In China, private NPOs have increasingly developed since the 2000s and acted to provide services for those in need. Cooperation with government grants the NPOs policy support, which is an indispensable requirement in the regulatory Chinese environment, as well as the opportunity for funding and influence. The government purchasing of services has promised profitable assignments for the organisations and incentivised a growing number of NPOs to engage in service provision for migrants. In Germany, both established organisations, such as the Welfare Associations and refugee councils, and also newer NPOs founded after the turn of the century, quickly adjusted existing service models to respond to the overwhelming needs of these newly arrived migrant populations in 2015. At the same time, multiple volunteer initiatives sprang up in Berlin and Cologne to fill the gaps left by existing services but, with the exception of some like the one German 'unsuccessful' case, many of these efforts did not continue after the initial crisis had passed.

In Germany, in all but two of the cases, NPOs self-initiated the projects and sought out cooperation with local government. Even in the case of the federally designed employment networks, the organisations engaged in the networks had a history of providing similar employment services and continued to offer supplemental services, not covered by the federal programme, to strengthen employment prospects. There are also Chinese cases where projects were initiated by NPOs, though in the majority of cases the government was responsible for the projects' initiation and the cooperation they involved, and in one case the government and an NPO took action jointly.

NPOs in all the cases engage in network governance. As explained by Levy and Ketels, this orientation towards long-term informal relationships, as opposed to bureaucratic structures, allows these NPOs to manage funding uncertainty and task complexity and to share specific knowledge and skills. There is much diversity in the scope and degree of networks observed in the 19 case studies, but they can be separated into organisations that are themselves networks, organisations that have built complex networks, German networks that explicitly exclude government and Chinese networks under the supervision of government agents. Network governance has a practical use for the NPOs, which depend on visibility, access to information and funding, cooperation partners and expertise. Particularly in China, good connections and contacts (*guanxi*) are important preconditions with which to successfully implement a project. In Germany, network governance is a central component of the social welfare system. It is rooted in Germany's corporatist tradition, as the Welfare Associations are organised as formal networks. Currently, service providers organise themselves into various networks, often according to policy areas and service types (Gluns, 2018; Grabbe, 2018).

As Lovelady and Grabbe as well as Ketels and Levy show, Coston's Model and Typology of Government–NPO Relationships (Coston, 1998) is a useful tool with which to capture the different cooperation models in the German and Chinese cases. With a few adaptions for the Chinese cases, it shows that there are a handful of dimensions that characterise the state–NPO relationship in terms of this cooperation. While outsourcing and networking are the main characteristics which underlie the whole sample of case studies, additional factors such as the formalisation of the state–NPO relationship, the linkage between the two actors as well as power structures in the relationship show great variety and determine very different kinds of cooperation. The nineteen case studies in the LoGoSO project display a variety of modes of cooperation from very informal and loose cooperation forms to highly formalised and interconnected cooperation. In China, the cooperation tends to be more formalised and the state exercises an authority that does not allow much autonomy on the side of the NPOs. The most obvious and hardly surprising difference between the German and Chinese cases is a stronger power asymmetry in favour of the state actors in the Chinese cases.

For the German cases, Lovelady and Grabbe identified that the networks range from more informal information-sharing bodies to formal bodies connected to specific policy goals. Network governance also plays an important role in the types of cooperative efforts the government and NPOs engage in. The very bureaucratic internal local public administration described by Zimmer and Grabbe means that government service provision is kept strictly within distinct policy areas. Participation in networks is a necessary element of the German social welfare system. In fact, as Lovelady and Grabbe highlight in the case of Kein Abseits!, representation in some formal networks, such as the youth welfare committees, is a prerequisite for receiving government funding. The nine German cases also show the level at which policy influences the types of government–NPO cooperation that occur. As Lovelady and Grabbe describe, among these cases, only in the area of employment is the government and NGO relationship the same in both Berlin and Cologne. In this instance, the migrant employment services are operated through a federal funded programme, which requires the formation of a local employment network that includes both public and private service providers. Employment is the only policy area in these case studies where policy is federally mandated. The other policy areas, social assistance, education and vulnerable groups, are predominantly decided at the state and local levels, and therefore cooperation models differ between the cities.

Local Government–NPO Cooperation: Factors that Influence the Cooperation

The LoGoSO project identified different factors that influence the local government–NPO cooperation cases that it observed and that determine their outcomes. Network governance appears to be the key to successful cooperation in all the German and Chinese cases. All the NPOs in the case studies developed networks with the government, but also with other NPOs, the media or companies and thereby managed to overcome many difficulties in their working environments. The 'unsuccessful' cases in China and Germany share the characteristic that their networks are either unsuccessful or underdeveloped.

Moreover, the case studies illustrate how cooperation with varying degrees of formalisation, linkage and power distribution can be successful, but they also reveal some limits. A competitive relationship without any linkage and qualitative connections between the state and an NPO can exist in the case of Germany; however, this cannot be considered an example of successful cooperation. In China, such a relationship would be problematic for the NPO and lead to restrictions as the government always assumes a high level of control. The Chinese cases of unsuccessful cooperation could not persist autonomously and ultimately were completely overruled by government structures. Levy and Ketels' analysis of the expression of third-party government criteria in the case studies shows that successful cooperation always depends on the existence of some kind of formalisation, as well as on the complementary distribution of functions and responsibilities in the cooperation. The criterion of a congruence of goals is an indispensable precondition for successful cooperation in China. As the state has a strong power advantage in every Chinese case, cooperation can only be successful if the NPO either pursues the same goals as the state or subordinates itself to the leadership of the authorities. The degree of power asymmetry in the Chinese cases depends on factors such as the NPO's field of work, governance and structure, as well as the advantages or disadvantages of particular individuals and their contacts with officials.

In Germany, the power relationship is more flexible and can even shift to a form of cooperation where the NPO does not have any power disadvantage against the state. Cooperation can therefore also be fruitful even if the NPO advocates different goals than the government. Also, the level of engagement in network governance may be key to successful cooperation. When the two youngest NPOs in the German cases are compared, there is a distinct difference in the ability of each to engage in a cooperative relationship with local government. On the one hand is Kein Abseits!, an organisation that is very network governance-oriented. Upon the organisation's formation, its staff joined all the key local networks and immediately began forming their own local, national and EU-level networks to further promote mentoring work. On the other hand, Be an Angel, an organisation very focused on service provision did not initially make any efforts to join official networks. This may be the reason for its failure in collaborating with the local government.

Results: Similarities and Differences between China and Germany

The overall results of the LoGoSO project show surprisingly striking similarities in the cooperation between local governments and NPOs to provide public services for migrants in China and Germany, but also distinct differences. In short, the similarities and differences can be summarised as follows:

State–Society Relations in Transformation: from Corporatism towards Neoliberalism

Both countries have a history of corporatist structures with the Welfare Associations in Germany and the GONGOs in China. They are now in a post-corporatist era influenced by principles of New Public Management. The cases of state–NPO cooperation in the service provision for migrants that were observed are characterised by a more neoliberal system.

The types of corporatism and the roles and conditions of NPOs differ in line with the different political systems in China and Germany. China builds on a tradition of authoritarian state corporatism and NPOs must navigate their way through a complex and restrictive regulatory system, while Germany grants freedom of association in its constitution and builds on liberal corporatism, which embraces plurality and freedom.

Challenges Posed by Migration: Local Government Responses

In both countries, the responsibility for integration falls heavily upon municipalities and the challenges faced by local administrations to provide responsive social services in the absence of adequate resources and expertise are similar.

The local governments in China had no experience with migration and were not prepared to integrate the migrating populations. Their efforts are still more focused on the creation and implementation of concepts, with the goal of integrating migrants into the social security system. In Germany, on the other hand, the municipalities have a long history of migration, and local policy is already focused on early integration strategies. The main need is the development of a service provision infrastructure which helps to pursue the goal of fully integrating the migrants into local society.

Challenges Posed by Migration: the Role of NPOs

In both countries, the local governments coordinate service provision with NPOs, and migrant integration services rely heavily upon NPOs.

In China, the involvement of NPOs in service provision is mostly regulated by the system of official government purchasing of services, while in Germany municipal integration policy incorporates elements of third-party government.

Local Government–NPO Cooperation: Models of Cooperation

In the majority of the Chinese and German cases, local governments are outsourcing migrant integration services to NPOs to harness NPO expertise and resources, provide public services and fulfil state and national requirements. From a bottom-up perspective, NPOs, in most cases, turn to cooperation with local administrations in an effort to engage in network governance to overcome difficulties in their working environment. The cooperation between government and NPOs is moreover characterised by factors such as formalisation of the cooperation and linkage between the actors and power structures involved, all of which show a great variety in both country samples.

In Germany, outsourcing is complementary and local government provides services in all the relevant policy areas, but those services are heavily supplemented by the work of NPOs. The projects are moreover mostly self-initiated by NPOs, who later sought out cooperation with local government. In China, migrant services in all four policy areas are completely outsourced to NPOs; in each area, the local government either cannot or will not provide the services needed. In the majority of (but not in all!!) the cases, the government is responsible for initiating schemes and for cooperating with NPOs. This cooperation also tends to be more formalised than in the German cases, and the Chinese state possesses and exercises much more power in that cooperation.

Local Government–NPO Cooperation: Factors that Influence Cooperation

In all the German and Chinese cases, network governance is the key to successful cooperation. The cases of 'unsuccessful' cooperation share the characteristic of badly developed or failed networks. Successful cooperation moreover depends on the existence of some kind of formalisation, as well as on the complementary distribution of functions and responsibilities in the cooperation.

In China, the government assumes a high level of control and has a strong power advantage in every example of cooperation. The cooperation can therefore only be successful if the NPO either pursues the same goals as the state or subordinates itself to the leadership of the state. In Germany, the power relationship is more flexible and can even shift to a form of cooperation where the NPO does not have any power disadvantage against the state. Cooperation can therefore also be fruitful even if the NPO advocates different goals than the government.

The comparison of "apples and pears" in this project, of the cooperation models between local governments and NPOs in Germany and China, shows that contemporary societies and local governments with different historical experiences and very different social, political and economic settings face similar challenges. It is the NPOs in these societies that complement the local administrations in the provision of services that address those challenges. This is the case in the field of migration, as this project has shown, but it is very likely also the case in similar global challenges, such as environmental degradation, climate change, poverty, and even questions of war and peace. The intention of this research project is to contribute to the understanding and recognition of the vital role NPOs play in a wide variety of different societies and areas of work.

References

Coston, Jennifer M (1998). "A Model and Typology of Government–NGO Relationships", *Non-profit and Voluntary Sector Quarterly*, 27:3, 358–382.

Gluns, Danielle (2018). "Refugee Integration Policy and Public Administration in Berlin" *LoGoSO Research Papers 6*, available online at https://refubium.fu-berlin.de/handle/fub188/22193.

Grabbe, Christina (2018). "Refugee Integration Policy and Public Administration in Cologne", *LoGoSO Research Papers 7*, available online at https://refubium.fu-berlin.de/handle/fub188/22775.

Grabbe, Christina (2020). "Education: RheinFlanke: HOPE", *LoGoSO Research Papers 20*, available online at https://refubium.fu-berlin.de/handle/fub188/26799.

Ketels, Anja (2019). "Migrant Integration as a Challenge for Local Governments and Social Organizations in China and Germany: Policy Traditions and Integration Measures in Guangzhou, Hangzhou, Berlin and Cologne", *LoGoSO Research Papers 8*, available online at https://refubium.fu-berlin.de/handle/fub188/24154.

Schönert, Carolin (2020). "Integration by education: Kein Abseits! e.V. Berlin", *LoGoSO Research Papers 21*, available online at https://refubium.fu-berlin.de/handle/fub188/26800.

Simon, Karla W. (2013). *Civil Society in China: The Legal Framework from Ancient Times to the "New Reform Era"*. New York: Oxford University Press.

Zimmer, Annette (1999). "Corporatism Revisited—The Legacy of History and the German Nonprofit-Sector", *Voluntas*, 10:1, 37–49.

Index